ETHICS IN BUSINESS

ETHICS IN BUSINESS

Thomas M. Garrett, S.J.

Sheed and Ward - New York

© *Sheed and Ward, Inc., 1963*

Library of Congress Catalog Card Number 63-17137

IMPRIMI POTEST:
   JOANNES M. DALEY, S.J.
   PRAEPOSITUS PROVINCIAE MARYLANDIAE

NIHIL OBSTAT:
   RT. REV. MSGR. JAMES T. CLARKE, S.T.L.
   CENSOR LIBORUM
   APRIL 10, 1963

IMPRIMATUR:
   ✠ JEROME D. HANNAN
   BISHOP OF SCRANTON
   APRIL 18, 1963

Manufactured in the United States of America

PREFACE

A GOOD BOOK on business ethics needs no defense. The present work, unfortunately, requires at least a word of explanation. Though written at the request of businessmen and with their aid, it makes little or no mention of many classic problems in business ethics. There are, for example, no chapters on pricing, wages or fair competition. Little is said of hiring and firing, commercial espionage or executive piracy. At the same time there are entire chapters devoted to the philosophy of work and such esoteric problems as psychological testing. As a result those who are accustomed to more conventional approaches may wonder what this book is supposed to do.

This book aims at enlarging the businessman's understanding of the nature and range of ethical problems involved in his work. It does not aim at solving all problems, but at stimulating their study. Perhaps it is best described as an invitation to businessmen and moralists to meet and develop answers to problems which demand a grasp of both principles and facts. A meeting of this sort is necessary, for the range of problems and principles is too great for any one man or any one group to handle all of them.

In addition to stimulating study, the book attempts to formulate some problems, to isolate areas that can be handled with ordinary principles and to point out problems which, because they are new, demand real research. This sort of work is very important, for unless we ask the right questions our answers are meaningless. In particular I have attempted to get at the sources of problems: attitudes, ideologies, creeds and social situations whose relation to the problems may not be explicitly recognized. A good deal of time and space has been devoted to these.

Where possible, I have indicated broad general principles which can solve the vast majority of cases in a given area. On the whole, no attempt has been made to treat the possible exceptions. There are two reasons for this. First, and most important, a lengthy treatment of the exceptions can often distract from the principles. At present it seems more important to lay a foundation than to do the interior decorating. Secondly, I hope in the future to write a case book of problems in business ethics, treating with the rarer and more subtle problems which can give rise to exceptions.

Anyone who scans the notes appended to each chapter will realize that this is the work not of a moral theologian but of an ethician, that is, of a man who is treating business problems in the light of reason. This seemed necessary since the problems are common to men of all faiths and of no faith at all. I wanted to supply a foundation which, though minimal in many respects, would be useful to everyone engaged in business. Catholic readers who wish to discover what the Church adds to the work of natural reason should study the Social Encyclicals and the work of the moral theologians.

Thomas M. Garrett, S.J.

Assistant Professor of Ethics

University of Scranton

ACKNOWLEDGEMENTS

THOSE WHO HAVE NEVER WRITTEN even a short book will smile at the acknowledgements which are an essential part of any preface. Authors, however, know that the real story is hidden in the list of names of those who helped. In my case particular thanks are due to Mr. Philip Scharper of Sheed and Ward, who encouraged me to write this book. In addition, I owe a debt of gratitude to the following who wrote long critiques of one or more chapters. I have not always followed their suggestions, but all of them have helped me to clarify my own thought. Professor John McLean of the University of Scranton, Raymond Baumhart of Loyola University, Joseph Haller of Georgetown University, Felix Cardegna of Woodstock College, Robert Springer of Fordham University, John Moonan of the Hibbert Printing Company, Douglas Murphy of Young and Rubicam, A. M. Sullivan of *Dun's Review*, Benjamin Masse of *America*. In addition, the following were kind enough to spend valuable time in discussing individual points. Wesley Wallace (Union Carbide), Clarence Walton (Columbia University), Frank Corbin (Milburn McCarthy Associates), Albert Tegler (Home Life Insurance Company of America), James Stabile (N.B.C.), Donald McGannon (Westinghouse Broadcasting), T. Edward Gavin (American Cyanamid), John Henderson (Henderson and Associates), Arthur Hull Hayes (C.B.S.), Tom W. Carr (Data Incorporated), Charles E. St. Thomas (Englehard Industries), and Joseph Kiely (Heinz).

Unless otherwise noted all citations are by permission of the publishers mentioned in the footnotes. Permission to quote from D. L. Munby's *Christianity and Economic Problems* has been granted by Macmillan and Co., Ltd., and St. Martin's Press. Harper and Row, who now hold the copyright for P. Drucker, *The Practice of Management,* and R. M. Allen, *Personality Assessment Procedures,* have been kind enough to authorize citations from these works. Passages reprinted from *Personnel* are by courtesy of the American Management Association; those from *Challenge: The Magazine of Economic Affairs,* by permission of the Institute of Economic Affairs, New York University. Special thanks are due to *America: The National Catholic Weekly Review* (920 Broadway, New York 10) for the citations from Samuel Y. Hyde and for the appendix by Raymond J. Murphy. The American Federation of Advertising holds the copyright to Morton Simon, *The Advertising Truth Book* (1960), which has been used through the kindness of Professor George Clarke, Education Director of the Federation. The material from Postley, *Computers and People* (1960), is reprinted by permission of the McGraw-Hill Book Company, Inc. The Massachusetts Institute of Technology Press is now the sole owner of Martin Greenberger (ed.), *Management and the Computer of the Future* (1962) and reserves all rights to itself.

CONTENTS

For Philip Land.

1 BUSINESS ETHICS AND BUSINESS ETHOS

QUESTIONS OF BUSINESS ETHICS are discussed not only in board rooms but at dinner tables, in university faculty rooms and on the floor of Congress. Of late, the topic has been treated not only by scholars but by professional associations. The schools and churches have renewed their interest in it too, and even the government has a Council of Advisors on Ethics to the Secretary of Commerce. For all this, it often seems that business ethics are like the weather, which everybody talks about but no one does anything about. Progress, however, is being made, though it has been impeded by misunderstandings about the nature of ethics, and by confusion about the nature of modern business. The general ethos of American society, as well as the special ethos of business, have contributed to this ambiguity and encouraged either despair or stereotyped thinking. As a result, any attempt to discuss business ethics must deal not only with particular problems but with a climate of uncertainty.

Ethical problems arise not only from the difficulty experienced in making a valid moral judgment, but from the practical obstacles to the execution of even a correct decision. A realistic study of business ethics must consider not only the principles to be applied but the human, cultural and institutional factors which influence their actualization. This seems particularly necessary in the United States where confusion about the nature

of ethics is rivaled, if not surpassed, by an understandable despair in the face of a complex and everchanging society.

Robert P. Sonnabend, writing in *Challenge*, put the problem
this way:

The essential dilemma arises from the fact that the Industrial Revolution undermined our ethical system. Although the world today is
different from that of 50 years ago and 100 years ago, we are still
learning ethics according to an ethos that vanished more than 300
years ago. We have not developed ethical concepts to deal with the
world of today, dominated as it is by speed, the development of the
organization and the revelation of nature's secrets. We know the phys-
iological reasons for birth and death. We know about space. We can
explain things that in bygone days were the mysteries of life. But our
ethical, moral and religious sense has not caught up with our scientific
and technological precocity.[1]

This is not to say that basic principles have changed but that
we are no longer sure how, and if, they apply to modern situations. Nor is it to say that the ethos determines what is right or
wrong, but that it definitely influences our ability to see what is
good or evil. This is particularly true in business where outmoded slogans drawn from outmoded economics and political
theory are shouted about with little concern for their moral
relevance in our present context. Indeed, as we shall see, false,
though unconsciously accepted, ideas about man, work, and
responsibility can and do tend to obscure the existence of real
problems.

In such a world we can no longer safely rely on the so-called
"conventional wisdom," much less on folkways and mores, or
current accepted practice. All these may once have enshrined
valid ethical conclusions, but a conclusion based on a given
historical situation may lose its relevance with the passage of
time. The only solution is to go back to basic principles and to

the existing reality in order to develop intermediate principles and practical conclusions which have real relevance and value.

The attempt to understand problems, and to develop a set of principles which are at once valid and applicable, is far from easy. Some cases are so complex that they almost seem to defy solution in terms of our present grasp of ethical principles. Though we must face these problems squarely, there is no room for moral despair. The majority of day by day problems are solvable; only a few are unique. It is important to recognize this, for some thinkers, hypnotized by the unusual and difficult case, have been tempted to deny the possibility of developing any principles or of finding any generalized solutions.

Ethics

Before attacking any concrete problems in the business world, it is necessary to remove some of the ambiguity which surrounds the idea of ethics. Ethics is not merely accepted practice inside an industry or profession, though it has to analyze the acceptance. Neither is it, as one businessman put it, what you can get away with and still keep the public quiet. Ethics certainly involves respect for the civil law, but it goes beyond this as well. Above all ethics must not be confused with what Professor Fletcher calls moralism, pietism, or legalism.[2] That is to say, it must not be confused with a purely personal or internal discipline, nor with petty precepts which leave large issues untouched. Again ethics can embrace many of these points, but it is not to be identified with them.

Ethics in the present work is taken to be the study of moral rightness and wrongness of human activity insofar as these can be known by reason. Such a study must consider nearly all aspects of man and his activity, but in relation to the ultimate and true good of man, not merely to what men want, or do, or think.[3] Ethics, then, is a human science, limited to a large extent by the state of our knowledge, but capable of arriving at some valid conclusions.

Here and there, one finds people of good will who believe that all ethical problems can be solved by a simple appeal to the golden rule, simple honesty or the conscience of noble men. They assume that man has some marvelous ability to intuit the good or evil of an act merely by looking at it. Unfortunately, the world as well as man is complex, and long hard work is required to find out what is good in the concrete and to form a conscience which is rational rather than emotional. Ethics must, in the real world, be concerned with helping men to make this investigation and to form correct judgments. It cannot content itself with a few simple rules of thumb. It must, if it is to give even relatively complete answers, devote some attention to the demands of society, the integrity of the individual and the relation between the two.

Such a task obviously involves a tremendous intellectual effort. Moreover, at the moment when rules and reason are to be applied to concrete cases, there is need for prudence. The magnitude of the task is well summed up by Land:

One is prudent who is willing to spend the time required to gain a full comprehension of the situation in which he must act and of those relationships, e.g., of consequence, which can be foreseen. He should possess a correct sense of the contingency of means and hence of their inadequacy and lack of scientific certitude. He must consequently undertake his investigation into means with a creativity which manifests care in deliberation. And this care will manifest itself in a thirst to be fully informed and consequently a willingness to seek counsel. It will show itself armed against impulsiveness and the temptation to grow weary of the task. It will be solicitous to gather a storehouse of experience.

To these "rules" we may add still others. The prudent man because he understands the inadequacy of means will be flexible about permitting change when he detects error, and he will allow for compensation to offset any undue emphasis discoverable in his prudential decisions. Yet he will not let inadequacy of means or any excessive caution frighten him off from tackling the situation which demands Maritain's "boldness," the courageous effort to make do with what one has to work with.[4]

Business Ethics

Business ethics is, then, an attempt to develop and apply basic principles in the area of human economic relations. Because of the nature of the field, business ethics has several particular qualities. More often than not, the problems in business are social, involving relations to groups as well as to particular individuals. Furthermore, the types of goods and evils involved, though not unimportant, generally do not have the same intrinsic significance as the goods and evils involved in medicine, criminal law, psychiatry and pastoral counseling. Often, we will be dealing with relative or physical goods rather than directly with absolutes. At the same time, business ethics are more than a type of commercial etiquette,[5] or a code of accepted practices. Although good ethics is certainly good business, our search is for principles and not merely for good business policy.[6]

Modern business ethics, because it must treat the problems of the giant corporation as well as those of the tradesman, peddler and small proprietor, must go into questions of social and political philosophy as well as into matters of truthfulness, exchange justice and fair treatment of employees. Indeed, so important is the corporation that much of what follows is focused on it rather than on the small business. Corporation ethics must give far more emphasis to the broader problems of social ethics than was customary at an earlier date.

This broad approach has been attacked in the past on the grounds that businessmen are not concerned with it. It may be that certain individuals are not aware of, much less interested in, this dimension. However, the problems do exist and should be met. In fact, it is precisely this area that, because it has been neglected, has brought charges of irresponsibility on the heads of business leaders. Any complete business ethics must consider the expectations of society, for these are part of the factual situation in which business exists. Even though these expectations may not be normative, they are often indications of the real needs of society, which business must fulfill to justify its existence. As A. A. Berle has noted, there is an unwritten contract between business and society as a whole.[7] The fulfillment of this contract, whose conditions are often expressed in social expectations, cannot be neglected without harm to both business and society.

This implies that the businessman must reexamine the traditional business creed and his own role in society. Undoubtedly, this will be a painful process, for the development of a sense of social responsibility will increase many of the strains inherent in the managerial function.[8] But the price of complacency and a happy reliance on old slogans may be even greater in the long run, and the re-examination is in order for pragmatic as well as moral reasons.

Like it or not, our knowledge and our judgments are conditioned by the ethos of our society.[9] The atmosphere of accepted but unquestioned values and attitudes which pervades a society gets into our thinking, colors it, limits it, blinds us to real issues. Such things as conformism, buck-passing, moral despair, or materialism do touch our lives, even when we do not embrace them as such. When the ethos is expressed in slogans used without thought, we can find it obscuring even basic agreements, so that they can no longer serve as a starting point for further cooperation. Thus old line battle cries such as "business is business" have served to hide the fact that modern business is much more than just business. Similarly, Fourth of July oratory about the free enterprise system can make us forget that the baby of free competition has grown up somewhat other than its parents planned. In other words, stereotypes supplied by the ethos can distort our vision not only of principles but of reality.

In view of the power of the ethos, it is necessary to question fundamental concepts in business ethics. Responsibility, the individual, work, society are all concepts which have been eroded with time and are yet central to the discussion of nearly all problems in both individual and social ethics. Indeed, a large number of interviews with businessmen have indicated that often their real uneasiness arises not so much from particular problems but from an inability to relate their work and decisions to a frame of reference large enough for all the dimensions of their life.

Case Work

Clarification of principles and concepts, though necessary, is not sufficient. A workable business ethics must demonstrate at least some of the methods for applying principles to concrete cases. Case work cannot solve all problems, but by providing some method of ethical decision making, it can ease the task, and free businessmen for careful consideration of those difficult cases which involve more than a routine application of principles. It is important to stress this since some writers have tended to over-emphasize the uniqueness of ethical questions to a point where there is little or no possibility of evolving set patterns of solution.

Granted all the difficulties inherent in developing an ethic in a sphere subject to constant change and obscured by myth and stereotypes, it is clear that men want and need answers.[10]

Answers in business ethics require mental and moral energy, but the task is worthy of both businessman and moralist, even if it results in no more than a clarification of issues.[11]

Some of the following chapters deal with broad general situations and principles. Some attempt to solve actual cases. A few deal with emerging problems while others rake over old ground. The studies of opinion making and waste in business are attempts to discover if, and to what extent, there *are* ethical problems in these areas.

This mixture of problems, perspectives and methods is deliberate. The aim is not so much to solve all problems, as to sketch approaches and to illustrate how the student of business ethics must go about his work.

Notes

1. Roger P. Sonnabend, "The Ethical Dilemmas of Businessmen," *Challenge,* January, 1962, p. 30; *cf.* Samuel S. Miller, "The Tangle of Ethics," *Harvard Business Review,* January-February, 1960 (vol. 38, no. 1), pp. 59-62.

2. Joseph Fletcher, "Situational Ethics: A Note for Business Management," *University of Washington Business Review,* October, 1960, pp. 18 ff.

3. *Cf.* Wayne A. R. Leys, "Attempting to Reduce Confused Nonsense of Business Ethics," *Business and Society,* Spring, 1961 (vol. 5, no. 2), pp. 5-9, for some interesting remarks on various meanings of business ethics.

4. *Cf.* Philip S. Land, S.J., "Practical Wisdom and Social Order," *Social Order,* November, 1955, p. 399.

5. *Cf.* James Melvin Lee, *Business Ethics* (Ronald Press, 1926), p. 176.

6. A. M. Sullivan, "Business Ethics: Policy or Principle," *Dun's Review and Modern Industry,* November, 1959.

7. A. A. Berle, Jr., "Unwritten Constitution for Our Economy," *The New York Times Magazine,* April 29, 1962, p. 7.

8. Francis X. Sutton, Seymour E. Harris, Carl Kaysen and James Tobin, *The American Business Creed* (Harvard University Press, 1956), pp. 303-383.

9. *Cf.* Cyril A. Zebot, "Ethos Patterns in a Competitive Society," *Review of Social Economics*, March, 1957 (vol. 15, no. 1), pp. 1-25.

10. *Cf.* Raymond C. Baumhart, S.J., "How Ethical Are Businessmen?" *Harvard Business Review*, July-August, 1961 (vol. 39, no. 4), pp. 6-19 and 156 ff., and "Ethics and Catholic Businessmen," *America*, January 6, 1962, pp. 436-438; February 3, 1962, pp. 589-591; April 14, 1962, pp. 47-52.

11. "Business Ethics: Too Much Grey Area," *Fortune*, September, 1960, pp. 127-128.

2 RESPONSIBILITY

THOSE WHO LIKE to put catchy tags on everything can hardly resist the urge to call the mid-twentieth century "the age of the buck-passer." Like all tags, this oversimplifies the problem, but it points to a profound truth. Today, no one is responsible for anything. The system is to blame. My drives are at fault. My environment has betrayed me. But I am not responsible. This might be amusing except that we have also seen the effects that flow from the easy sluffing off of obligation and the sense of duty. The great T.V. scandals that made payola a household word in 1959, and the sentencing of the G.E. and Westinghouse officials for price-fixing in 1961, occasioned brilliant, if unsuccessful, displays of buck-passing, lame self-defense and the easy acceptance of the easy excuse.

When the T.V. scandals first broke, no one in authority even admitted knowing about them; let alone would anyone accept the responsibility for them. Some of those most deeply involved swore oaths to their ignorance and innocence. Then came a period of defense and dramatized *shame at being caught*. Some groups justified themselves on the grounds that payola was an accepted industry practice. For others it was a necessity. For yet a third group it was moral because it did not hurt anyone. Few cared to bow their heads and admit that any real wrong had been done, though some of those who pleaded innocence also promised to clean house. Indeed, the lack of moral convictions which appeared in the wake of the scandals was almost more alarming than the rigged quiz shows themselves.

The price fixing scandals in the electrical industry were perhaps even more alarming. Here it was not a question of "two-bit operators", or of borderline professions, but of the pillars of society. Yet the pleas of "not guilty" had a familiar ring. Top management claimed to be ignorant of what subordinates had been doing. Subordinates felt that they were acting with tacit approval. The lawyers' plea that a sentence would be unjust, only served to prove Judge Ganey's opinion that the great electrical conspiracy "was a shocking indictment of a vast section of our economy."[1]

Most alarming of all is the fact that the basic moral attitudes manifested in both these cases bear a close resemblance to that of the Nazi war criminals who excused themselves on the ground that they were following orders or policy. Judge Ganey seems to have been aware of this when he spoke of "the company man, the conformist, who goes along with his superiors and finds balm for his conscience in additional comforts and the security of his place in the corporate setup." In other words, there was a real moral weakness at the root of the whole problem.

During all this time there was a great deal of head wagging and viewing with alarm, but the general public and professional circles did not take many effective steps to remedy the situation. The Federal Communications Commission received only a nominal number of complaints from the public at large. Indeed, those advertising and television executives who felt the whole thing would blow over, seem to have been on very safe ground. All this indicates that the lack of responsibility extends beyond those whose names were splashed across the headlines.

None of this need really surprise us since the failure to face responsibility is a commonplace of American life. The failures of school children are blamed on their emotional problems. The criminal is viewed as a victim of environment, while the adulterer can blame his drives or his spouse. The currency of such terms as irresistible impulse, complex and unconscious drive indicates the new view of responsibility. The fact that they are heard and invoked nearly everywhere shows that the problem of responsibility is common to both business and society as a whole.

Roots of the Evil

Though we do not want to imply that all sense of responsibility has disappeared in American life, we must face the fact that a variety of things have served to weaken it. Since responsibility is basic to all ethics, and since the problem is so widespread, we have to understand the roots of it before assigning duties or suggesting remedies. This is all the more necessary since in some cases, and especially in business, the causes are objective and institutional as well as subjective and personal.

At the risk of oversimplifying and exaggerating, it must be said that a large part of our population lives in an atmosphere of Sunday Supplement Determinism. Popularized Freudianism and Behaviorism have seeped through the mass media, the classroom and the cocktail party, until large numbers have adopted a pseudoscientific contempt for both free will and moral obligation. After all, why believe in something so inconvenient as responsibility if popular science provides us with the perfect excuse for avoiding it? It suits men without any real system of values to believe that they cannot control their drives and are really puppets manipulated by the unconscious. Why bother about old fashioned restraint and stick-to-itiveness, if it is all an illusion anyway? Why face the world when the giant mechanisms of society will only crush me, if I raise a voice in protest?

While such a caricature will not find its way into serious

literature, something like it is in the air and influences a great deal of thinking. Even though the distortions of science *are* distortions, they have a genuine effect, especially on those who are looking for a way out. Add to these false ideas a fear of manipulation, anxiety about mythical hidden persuaders and brain washers, and you can understand the confusion and paralysis which grip so many people. There is a feeling of being really helpless and hopelessly caught up by forces too terrible to name and too strong to resist.

These exaggerations and fears do not operate unaided. They are supported by the new gospel of social adjustment and conformism which seems to have sprung not only from the psychology of adjustment, but from an extreme concept of democratic living.[2] The prevalence of the peace of mind books is one sign of the worship of adjustment, while the Organization Man might almost be the symbol of the whole movement towards conformity. Here too, we find the "group think," and the classification of men according to the statistical averages, so beloved of the psychological testing services.

While not everyone succumbs to these pressures, the temptation is strong. Children are told to be like the others and encouraged to follow the group. To be superior or different is to fail in social living. Our adults are pressured into exalting the oldest of lame excuses, "Everybody is doing it." Anyone who objects is silenced with the great principle of moral relativism: "Who are you to say what is right or wrong?" As a result it is hard to think for oneself, to stand up for principle or to make one's own choices; correspondingly easy to flee from choice, responsibility and the cruel necessity of making up one's own mind.

All this is quite obviously part and parcel of the new ethic which reduces morals to folkways and mores, rejects all fixed standards and tosses sanction out of the house. Ethics is now only a question of accepting social standards, not of following a code that has ultimate validity and meaning. When this is coupled with the decline in real religious influence and the breakdown of the Protestant ethic of self-reliance, even the philosophic basis of responsibility has been sapped.

These ideas probably would not have caught on and spread if social conditions had not provided a seed ground. In the first place, the rapidity of social change has left people bewildered, faced with problems which the old ethic did not cover explicitly, or caught up in a world where competition and not principle is supposed to rule. The natural moral leaders have failed to point the way, and the enticing prospect of an easy out and no responsibility has filled the vacuum. As the pace of change increases and tensions mount, the desire to escape turns into a real flight from self-determination.

Some observers feel that this has been complicated by our new abundance which has, if nothing else, softened the American character. The young, having been brought up without the struggle of either the frontier or the depression years, are supposed to be flabby. Even if this is not true, it is clear that many in our society believe that life should not be hard. For them, suffering and sacrifice and the agony of self-control are impositions, obstacles to be avoided at any cost. Obviously enough, a sense of responsibility can hardly flourish in such an atmosphere.

The conflicts and confusions resulting from social change have been carefully described by the Gordons, in their book *The Split Level Trap*.[3] Even those who shudder at the advice which the Gordons give can still recognize the validity of their case histories. Many of the mobile families they describe are beset by a feeling of hopelessness and inability to cope with life in the new suburbia. The result of such despair is almost inevitably a loss of responsibility, for responsibility implies the ability to control one's own life.

These confusions and conflicts are really only part of a larger and more deep seated confusion resulting from the speed and complexity of modern social life. The government moves away from us as it grows bigger, and the complexity of the issues involved in public life staggers even the experts. The result is often a sort of cynicism and defeatist attitude expressed in such phrases as: "Why vote, when the politicians have decided everything ahead of time?" "Why even try when one man can do nothing?" "Why bother?" "What's the use?" "Who cares as long as they leave us alone!"

All of this has also led to a new sort of depersonalization. Society is so big that we can no longer have personal experience of more than a narrow slice. So we resort to statistical descriptions and statistical justifications of our actions. We tend to see ourselves as only a single bee in a hive, one ant in the ant hill, except in those rare moments when we are in our own home. Indeed, outside the narrow circle of friends and family we feel ourselves to be strangers, ciphers, no more than faces lost in the crowd. In such an environment we almost necessarily are tempted to give up hope of being ourselves or ruling our lives.

In the Business World

Business is only a part of the world around us. Its leaders breathe the same atmosphere and are victims of the same errors and rationalizations as the rest of men. As a matter of fact, they must face in intensified form the temptations we have described: for the big corporations demand a conformity, mobility and self-surrender that further dilute the sense of responsibility. This does not mean that there is no warmth, decency, or human feeling in business. Human qualities are present to a degree that would surprise the outsider. But the demands of corporate citizenship do weaken the sense of real responsibility.

Some large corporations are almost a way of life. They offer not only employment but a sort of psychological security that comes from belonging to the group. Andrew Hacker has described the situation as follows:

By now we all know about the social facilities provided by large corporations. Eastman Kodak's medical plan, I.B.M.'s country clubs, Richfield Oil's model homes, du Pont's psychiatrists, Reynolds Tobacco's chaplains, and even R.C.A.'s neckties with their corporate insignia—all of these are symptomatic of the concerted effort to create a feeling of community within the corporation. They have been brought about in large part because the middle-class employee has no alternative community to which he can find a sense of belonging.[4]

These efforts have had phenomenal success in many cases. The dedicated G.M. executive can speak of that sprawling corporation with almost religious fervor. Some among them feel that they owe an allegiance equivalent to the chauvinistic motto, "My country right or wrong, but my country." One does not criticize the upper levels even when they are wrong, for the company cannot survive without loyalty. Indeed, in some few cases the obedience is greater than that which a religious superior would dare to demand from a subject.

In many cases the company even tends to swallow up the home life of the executive. The idea is to create such an attitude in the wife that even she is willing to admit that her husband belongs to the corporation.[5] If and when companies succeed in building up such over-all loyalty, they can count on an absence of the conflicts which might make an executive critical. This in its turn would seem to weaken a man's ability to think for himself when moral problems arise.

While all these factors serve to weaken a critical sense of responsibility, the very nature of the large corporation is probably an even more potent factor. Big business is complex not only in structure, but in its effects on individuals and society. Like society itself, the corporation and corporation law are changing so rapidly that old norms no longer give clear answers. Indeed, the businessman is at present so beset by conflicting role expectations that it is difficult for him to know exactly where his responsibilities lie. The law expects him to work primarily for the good of the stockholders or owners. Unions expect him to give top consideration to the welfare of the workers. Local communities often expect firms to stay, even when profit considerations demand a change of plant location. Unless these facts are kept in mind, our treatment of business responsibility may end up abstract and utopian.

Writers such as A. A. Berle have given us a clear picture of that business world where power and property are divided in such a way that it is not clear who is responsible for the acts of the corporation.[6] Since the legal owners are often other corporations with equally complex organizational setups, the map of responsibility needs to be recharted. Even inside individual businesses, it may be hard to discover who has the power and so the responsibility for the activities of the group. When decisions are made by boards, consultants, and groups, rather than individuals, it becomes easy to dodge many responsibilities: for you can always pass the blame on to some faceless committee.

Some would like to solve the problem by saying that the president of the company must take full responsibility and that others need not bother too much about such fine ethical questions. This is unrealistic, for underlings have their area of independence and their influence on upper level decisions. Policy written or unwritten is supposed to determine the areas of competence, and granted that there are large grey sections, the fact of power and responsibility remains. Policy, unfortunately, can also be another escape for the man who views himself as a bureaucrat making routine decisions according to the book. Indeed, the bureaucratic morality, based on impersonal policy, may be one of the real causes of the flight from responsibility. As we shall see in our chapter on Automation and Management Decision, the mechanization and rationalization of the office will probably lead to an increase of this type of thinking and the consequent diffusion of a sense of duty.

While the man at the top may seem in a position to clarify many of these issues, we must remember that he too is a human being, subject to manifold pressures. If he is weak, he may seek to hide his own power behind the anonymity of the committee, the group or the chain of command. Even when he is not a victim of such frailty, he may still be in a position where he cannot get a decision carried out. Thus, though General Electric's top executives prohibited price agreements with competitors (in general instruction 2.35), men lower in the hierarchy failed to comply with this directive.

Even if the lines of power were absolutely clear, the businessman would still have to face the fact that it is not clear how his various responsibilities balance out. Even a top executive is responsible to the stockholders, the board, the public, the nation, to his employees, to the company as a separate entity and to his own person. While it is easy to say that he must bring all of these into harmony with each other, the doing is another question.

In attempting to reconcile his responsibility to all these groups, the businessman is also faced with the fact that his conscience may tell him to do one thing, the law another, and current business practice yet a third. Moreover, when he is engaged in a power struggle not only with his competition but with the government and the labor unions, he may be tempted to sacrifice principle to expediency. In short, the situation is so difficult that there is a real and even understandable temptation to give up.

All these difficulties are great enough even in the abstract. In the concrete they are further complicated because the businessman is not always able to foresee the effects of his acts or to distinguish accidental from essential. After all, the businessman is a warrior against uncertainty and risk. Ignorance, guess work and prudence are at the very center of his work. No one should be surprised if he does not know exactly what consequences to expect from a given course of action. Yet, he is really responsible only for what he can foresee and control, and not always then. This sort of difficulty will be illustrated in our chapter on selling and waste in modern economies. For now, suffice it to say that this ignorance of effects is often a cause of failure to be concerned with the broader levels of responsibility.

In simpler societies with a slow rate of change, many of these problems do not exist, or exist on a much smaller scale. Indeed, in those communities, long experience has given the businessman a fair idea of what he should and should not do. There may even be an accepted code of action which covers most situations, so that there is no need for constant investigation and readjustment. Today, however, even the law is so confused that the businessman often has to guess at its meaning and act according to his own interpretation. In his book, *The Language of Dissent*,[7] Mason says that he advises the client to act not in accord with the law, but in accord with what the bureaucrat will think the law is, in a given time and place. Similarly, the public may think a course of action is harmful while management thinks it necessary. Since neither side knows for sure the actual effects and actual morality, everyone feels free to act as he pleases.

This type of uncertainty breeds more confusion and disputes. The public often assumes that the businessman is the cause of some evil which he had nothing to do with. At other times, management is asked to assume control of affairs where it has no competence. The result is simply that management stops listening to the do-gooders, who are living in a world all their own. When this type of situation is multiplied over and over again it becomes almost impossible to work out the ethics of new situations. As we shall see in our discussion of the opinion makers, the critics and reformers are often hiding from their own responsibilities at the very moment they are attacking big business and its advertising agents. Is it any wonder that management often resigns itself to following the mob, or its own whim, in ethical matters?

In the last place, we must return to one of the fundamental theses of this book. In the absence of any grounded public consensus as to moral norms, the goals of society, the function of business and the hierarchy of purposes, the business world is of necessity battered by the conflicting opinions of do-gooders, reformers, liberals, conservatives and what have you. In other words business is often left without the help and support of the community at large.

This lack of public consensus is, of course, part of the much larger problem of cultural and ethical pluralism. For all that, it cannot be disregarded in its particular aspects, since it has a rather direct bearing on the problem of business responsibility. There are thinkers who believe that business has no right to make decisions in the name of society which will have important impact on society and the economy. Others see in the new social consciousness of business a threat to political processes and political freedom.

The point is simply this. Because of the disagreement about the nature of business and the limits of its social responsibilities, attempts to exercise too much of a sense of duty may lead to violent disputes and even government regulation. In the face of such fears, and beset by such a lack of coherent political and social theory, business is tempted to do only what it is forced to do, or what it finds profitable. Or to put it another way, the confused state of public opinion can make too much responsibility a luxury which few companies can afford.

Progress and More Problems

Despite all these difficulties both in business and in society at large, progress has been made. Perhaps it is merely a result of enlightened self-interest, but leaders in the field of business have become acutely aware of the problem of responsibility. One need only read such magazines as the *Harvard Business Review, Fortune* or *Personnel*, to become aware of this trend. Some even feel that the days of "the public be damned" are gone forever. While this may be over-optimistic, it is true that the businessman often speaks of his duties and pays at least lip-service to higher ideals.

All of this is well and good, even if we do not know how deep or how widespread the convictions actually are. Surveys by the *Harvard Business Review* are not always too helpful in this area, since the readers of that magazine represent one of the most socially advanced segments of the business world. Even if the new concern with the public and with the employee were universal and sincere, we would still have to face the problem of perfectionism. As Benjamin M. Selekman has pointed out, the executive can promise to do too much and fail in his essential duty by becoming over-involved in matters beyond his competence. He writes as follows:

I fear that spokesmen for American Industry may be in danger of giving an impression of managerial competence not warranted by the present state of knowledge, and of making commitments to ethical standards impractical of realization in the here and now.[8]

A few illustrations of Mr. Selekman's thesis will show the extremes which must be avoided in working out the responsibilities of the businessman. If management decides that it is responsible for the human happiness of its workers, it may be distracted from the main work of production and end up without either profit or any increment in human relations. Of course, the work environment should be as satisfactory as possible, but what we may call therapeutic work seems, at present, to belong to others. Similarly no businessman can afford to get too far ahead of his competition in fulfilling social responsibilities, without risking the ruin of his company and eventual harm to society.

In the long run so many of these problems are beyond the immediate power of any one group, that it would be folly to attempt to do it alone. In other words ideals must be aided by prudence lest goodwill destroy itself.

Though there is much good sense in Mr. Selekman's position, the danger of perfectionism is overshadowed by the temptations we have catalogued in the first pages of this chapter. Perhaps American Catholics are particularly prone to perfectionism since all too few of them have taken the time to think out the practical means which must be used to realize the ideals set out in the social teaching of the Church. Indeed, the starry-eyed idealism of much Catholic writing is so far removed from the real order of things that it has been shrugged off by those in a position to do something about it.

A second sign of progress is the frequent insistence that business schools give their students an awareness of the social significance of business and its ethical responsibilities. Again, however, we are faced with the distinct possibility that this may be another example of lip service and wishful thinking.

As William H. Whyte has noted in *The Organization Man*, the trend is not without a countertrend which is strongly and narrowly vocational, not to say pragmatic.[9] Despite pious protestations, the recruiter is liable to pick the technician rather than the well-rounded student. As one such agent put it to me: "All other things being equal, I will pick the young man with the liberal background." How often, however, are all other things equal, if you have not had the technical courses? The result is that many schools continue to give trade courses with only the tiniest sprinkling of the liberal approach.

Courses and education, however, are probably not the answer, for a far more profound reason. Our educators suffer from the same confusion about values that marks the population as a whole. More often than not, the ethics are relativistic and without firm roots, while the social policies run arbitrarily from socialistic to mild *laissez faire* doctrines. No need to be surprised by this. After all these same educators must bear some of the blame for the situation that actually exists. In brief, education, at least of the kind we are familiar with, is not likely to play the decisive role that some have attributed to it.

Basic Responsibilities

The first obligation of the man in business is to face the problem of responsibility as it actually exists, not only in business, but in society. Until he faces up to these manifold aspects and strips himself of all rationalizations, there is little hope that he will do anything more. At the same time, he must recognize that the effort to face responsibility in business involves a corresponding effort in other departments of his life. So long as a man's private life is in tatters, it is not to be expected that he will face the problems of business with constancy and courage.

In confronting the problem as we have outlined it, the thoughtful executive must come to the conclusion that to a large extent only the professional can say the last word on the problem of responsibility. The ethician can help him in straightening out his values, and in seeing the dimensions of the problem. The economist, political scientist and sociologist may even supply him with useful information, but in the last analysis the business leader himself must put the various aspects together and decide the limits of his responsibility in concrete situations. The reason for this is simple. Only the man in the field knows enough about the facts of the case to make a truly prudential judgment. All others are outsiders who are liable to overlook important factors, to over-simplify or to miss entirely that subtle climate of opinion and congeries of expectations which, though subjective in origin, exert a great influence on the objective order.

The foregoing obligation is almost too much for the individual to shoulder since it demands a competence which few possess. As a consequence, there is going to be a subsidiary obligation to join with others who have a similar problem in order to pool efforts and work out answers. This point is taken up in our chapter on professional organizations and need not be developed here. Suffice it to say, however, that even the professional group will find this a difficult duty to fulfill.

Neither of the first two obligations can be fulfilled unless the individual has a high degree of technical competence in his own field. This is the modern way of saying that every man has duties of his state in life. These duties include competence simply because the good of society depends on the ability of those who direct the economy and fulfill subsidiary functions in it. To put it another way, the public good demands that the individual develop his talents within his work and sphere of activity. This implies that one's position in the business world is not an indifferent matter, for though the individual may be content with his development, society may be suffering because of his laziness or lack of ambition.

This, of course, brings us back to the problem of work and the need to overcome a false otherworldliness so characteristic of certain groups of good Christians. If the "good men" have neither power nor competence, the "bad men" will run the world. Christian humility and detachment may justify a lack of interest in comfort and advancement as such, but they cannot justify a failure to use one's ability for the good of other men. The admirable desire to be a good father may cause a man to limit his work, but if this carries him away from facing and accepting broader responsibilities, there is something unrealistic about his set of values.

Almost inevitably, the previous paragraphs bring us back to one of the great basic facts of the moral life. Doing the right thing is not necessarily easy. Or to put it another way, virtue may be its own reward, but there is a price to pay for it. In particular the acceptance of responsibility involves the acceptance of sacrifices and suffering. Though this seems almost trite, there are so many who fight against this conclusion that it needs to be emphasized. Even good Christians bridle at the thought that there is a price to pay for principle and that good intentions are not enough if one dodges the uncomfortable aftermaths of having taken a stand.

When a man is in the higher ranks of management it is particularly important that he take a stand, for in business as elsewhere example is a powerful force. Raymond C. Baumhart reports on a basis of some two thousand replies to a questionnaire that:

Close examination of our data reveals a tendency in every age group, company milieu, and management level to accept the values of his superiors. This tendency, stemming from a respect for the talents of the superior as well as from his authoritative position, should be acknowledged by every administrator as part of his power for good or evil.[10]

Though the influence of one's peers for ethical behavior seems to be weak, it is relatively important in influencing unethical conduct. This means that good example has a prophylactic effect with regard to one's equals even though it may not lead them on to the heights. Admittedly, there is nothing new in this, but it is interesting to note that contemporary studies confirm the ancient principles about the evils of scandal.

Since the roots of irresponsibility are found in society and in the value systems of individuals, there is also a more general obligation to work quietly and peacefully for an improvement in this area. There should be no illusions about the possibility of immediate success. Executives in the communications industry, for example, estimate that it may take a full generation to educate the owners of radio and television stations to a sense of their obligations. It takes no great wisdom to see that this is not a job for the boyish enthusiast or for the unordained preacher. Only a prudent and patient man can hope to fulfill this responsibility effectively.

Good example, of course, is not merely a question of pious exhortations or protestations of principle. It must extend to the area of action. This is terribly threadbare as a principle, yet recent business history indicates its importance. In analysing the great electrical conspiracy, the Editors of *Fortune* noted that though company policy forbade price fixing, it also made such demands on subordinates to produce or else, that it nullified itself. While this may be put down to a failure in communication or in human relations, it may also be charged to a lack of effectively implemented moral direction. At worst it is a sort of corporate hypocrisy, for subordinates seem to have known that if they did not play ball they would be replaced. In a word, the executives found themselves crushed between official policy and actual practice, as well as between technical expediency and private conscience.

All of this implies that the businessman must not accept the status quo with its excuses both real and imaginary for avoiding responsibility. Things are not going to change themselves, and ethics demands not merely a passive conformity to one's principles, but a real effort to create a milieu in which those principles have meaning for others. Indeed, everything that has gone before can be summed up as an obligation to create situations in which morality can flourish.

Limits of Responsibility

Even though one may not accept obstacles passively, the fact remains that any prudent estimate of one's responsibilities here and now, must take the limitations into consideration. Insofar as responsibility and power go together, a man cannot hold himself responsible for what he cannot change or control. At a given minute a given individual cannot change the whole of business, let alone society. To attempt to do so would court failure and probably set up road blocks to future progress. There is room then for a careful evaluation of the *possible* when considering means to the *ideal*. Thus, when the evils to be avoided are not intrinsic, and the good to be accomplished is not absolutely necessary, there is often room for temporary toleration of evil in view of a greater good. Thus low wage levels can sometimes be permitted for a time when a sudden rise would, by dislocating the economy, harm everyone. So too, it may sometimes be momentarily permissible to put up with less desirable trade practices until such time as they can be changed without disrupting existing contracts.

When it is a question of the social responsibilities of business, there is nearly always a question of who has the major responsibility. As a rule, the government, the public, and other groups play a role, and the businessman need not take the whole burden on himself, so long as he faces the fact that he still has some duties.

In estimating his responsibility, the businessman ought to remember that most of his activities have more than one effect. Indeed, there are few activities that do not have at least some harmful results. Shifting a plant location can increase profits, create employment and contribute to more efficient production, but it can also cause dislocations in a community and cause some people to lose their jobs. Advertising which helps some people to shop more intelligently can tempt others to spend more than they can afford. An increase in one company's sales may spell bankruptcy for another firm.

Obviously, no one can be obligated to avoid all the harmful effects of his actions, since this would render action itself almost a moral impossibility. It is necessary, however, to evaluate the situation very carefully before coming to a decision, and this may even necessitate the services of a professional moralist. Here, we will merely indicate some of the classic principles which must be brought to bear on the decision.

In the first place a man is only obliged with regard to those results which he can reasonably foresee. This point is so obvious that it hardly needs mentioning. However, reasonable foresight does imply that a man has considered the possible effects of his acts. Deliberate ignorance or neglect of normal investigations is no excuse.

Secondly, when a particular business activity has both good and bad effects, there is room for the principle of multiple effect.[11] According to this principle a man may permit an evil effect which he foresees, but does not intend, if the immediate good effects of his activity counterbalance the evil. The word "permit" is important because it implies that the evil is not willed as either a means or an end. Moreover, if the evil is a means by its very nature, and not merely a concomitant, this principle cannot be used, for the end cannot justify the means.

Let us illustrate these points with a few examples. Cutting prices below costs in an effort to drive a competitor out of business is immoral, not only because the immediate means is unjust, but because such a course of action involves *willing* harm to another. On the other hand, *legitimate* price reductions, designed to serve the consumer and increase business, could justify our permitting the other dealer to suffer financial loss. The harm stemming from plant relocation could be permitted if the new location would considerably improve the economic position of the company by bringing it closer to raw materials and a market. It would be different, however, if the increased profitability was a result of *exploiting* cheap labor in the new market.[12]

Obviously real cases are far more complicated than this. Often it is difficult to decide whether the good is equal to the harm or whether the evil is being used as a means. These difficulties are common to most moral problems and merely point up the need for careful evaluation of both ethical principles and factual situations.

To Whom Is Business Responsible

The businessman stands at the center of a network of relationships. His decisions affect the public, the government, the company, stock holders, employees, the industry of which he is a part, and the business community as a whole. In an ideal order, the interests of all these parties would automatically be in harmony with sound values, but in the real world they must be brought into order and balance so that all are well served. Often there are real conflicts, and in the absence of legal provisions, the executive must decide whose interests take precedence, and to what extent.

There is no easy way to make these decisions. Each case involves many principles and such a variety of circumstances that a set of stock answers can be dangerous. Moreover, before any attempt is made to present even the basic principles it is necessary to clarify the nature of business and its relation to individuals and society. To put it another way, we must understand business before we can understand the nature of its responsibilities.

Notes

1. *Cf.* Richard Austin Smith, "The Incredible Electrical Conspiracy," *Fortune,* April, 1961, pp. 132-137; 172ff., and May 1961, pp. 161-164; 210ff.
2. *Cf.* William H. Whyte, Jr., *The Organization Man* (Doubleday Anchor Books, 1957) and David Riesman *et al., The Lonely Crowd* (Yale University Press, 1950).

3. Richard E. Gordon, Katherine K. Gordon and Max Gunther, *The Split-Level Trap* (Bernard Geis Associates, 1961).

4. Andrew Hacker, *Politics and the Corporation* (Fund for the Republic, 1958), p. 8.

5. William H. Whyte, Jr., *Is Anybody Listening?* (Simon and Schuster, 1953), p. 146.

6. Adolf A. Berle, Jr., *Power Without Property* (Harcourt, Brace and Co., 1959).

7. Lowell Mason, *The Language of Dissent* (World Publishing Co., 1959), p. 20. The author, for eleven years a member of the Federal Trade Commission, gives an all too vivid picture of the difficulties raised by administrative law.

8. Benjamin M. Selekman, "Sin Bravely: The Danger of Perfectionism," *Harvard Business Review,* January-February, 1959, p. 105.

9. Whyte, *The Organization Man,* pp. 109-110.

10. Raymond C. Baumhart, "Problems in Review: How Ethical Are Businessmen?" *Harvard Business Review,* July-August, 1961, p. 156.

11. For a more closely reasoned examination of this principle of double effect consult the moralist, or Herbert Johnston, *Business Ethics* (Pitman Publishing Co., 1956), pp. 114-117.

    For further reading consult John F. Cronin, *Social Principles and Economic Life* (Bruce, 1959), especially pp. 143-164; Howard R. Bowen, *Social Responsibilities of the Businessman* (Harper and Brothers, 1953). This last is a publication of the Federal Council of Churches and worthwhile reading.

12. *Cf.* Henry J. Wirtenberger, S.J., *Morality and Business* (Chicago: Loyola University Press, 1962), pp. 38-40, for some general principles on morality and responsibility.

3 MAN, BUSINESS AND SOCIETY

THE CONFUSION SURROUNDING the notion of responsibility and its application to business is, in large part, only a reflection of blurred and shifting ideas about the nature of man, of business and of society. Ultimately, every problem in business ethics involves these three elements. If a man's concepts are seriously defective, not to say false, the chances of making a correct judgment are small. Of course, some refuse to take a stand on these points and are content to follow the customs and practices of their neighbors. Such people may be right occasionally, but they are on dangerous ground in a society where customs are often the result of emotional reactions rather than carefully thought-out principles.

A reasoned stand on these three points is necessary not only to insure correct decisions, but to lessen those strains that arise when the manager confuses personal relations with relations of authority.[1] Only a correct philosophy of man, business and society can enable the executive to evaluate his various roles as a human person, as a manager with authority, and as a citizen.

Such a philosophy will not solve all problems. It is not intended to do so. It can, however, orient the businessman to the questions, and help him to think them through.

Even such a limited goal is not easy to reach. The ethos of the business world contains some strange ideas. The old tenets of utilitarianism and classical economic theory jostle with contemporary talk of social responsibility. Words like stewardship and paternalism and laissez-faire are less popular than the term human relations, but the old ideas are around even though they have changed their names. Along with this, one still finds the concept of man the creator fighting the theory of man the irrational: a being motivated only by self-love, power or profit. Here and there, the businessman may even stumble across those who would subject the individual completely to the social economy.

There is confusion about the nature of business too. Profit is the goal of business, cry some. Others say profit is simply the necessary means to the survival of firms. "Business is the support of all that is good and noble!" "Business is the monster which is ruining our culture!" "Business is a hard cold world apart!" "Business is a home away from home!" These are among the conflicting philosophies that beat upon the ears of employer and employee alike. It is no wonder then, that a reorientation will be difficult.

Judeo-Christian Idea of Man[2]

Despite the verbal confusion about man, there is, in American society, an underlying consensus about his nature. Often this is obscured by the current ethos, or sacrificed to expediency, but it is there nevertheless. Even those who profess to be agnostics, will, when pressed, frequently end up by accepting much, if not all, of the Judeo-Christian idea of man. The reasons are simple enough. First, all our social and political institutions are based on this idea. Second, it corresponds to even the common sense knowledge we have of ourselves. Third, it has, in the course of history, received adequate philosophic justification and, despite its theological origins, can to a large extent stand on the basis of reason alone.

No attempt will be made here to justify this idea of man. Time and space permit only an outline of the aspects most pertinent to business ethics. Unless there is agreement on these basic points, it would be necessary to write an introduction as large as the New York Telephone Directory.

Man is the image of God. All created things exist for him, and society as well as business must ultimately be ordered to his well-being and growth. The person, precisely as a person, is never a means, a thing, a commodity, or an article of commerce. We cannot be indifferent to the way our acts affect other men without being indifferent to ourselves. Indeed, our own welfare is so bound up with that of others that any injury to a neighbor ultimately becomes an injury to ourself.

These ideas need to be refined, but the basic principles must be affirmed vigorously since our constant temptation is to forget our dependence on others and the sacred nature of man.

When we take a longer look at man, we are struck not only by his complexity (he is a being enmeshed in a network of relationships), but by the fact that not all relationships or parts of man are equal in value. Man has body and mind, will and intellect, feelings and activity. He is a social being, an island at times, but one washed by many waters. Even in society, he plays a variety of roles, speaks a multitude of idioms. All these relationships are not equally necessary for his well-being. All, however, are ordered to the total good of man and to his ultimate perfection.

Much of this may sound poetical if not mystical until we examine what the statements mean in actual situations. We recognize that it is legitimate and even necessary to sacrifice an arm or an eye to save the life of man. This is to say that these goods are subject to the good of the whole. So too a man sells his labor as an object but does not sell himself. The labor can be treated as a means but the man cannot. We recognize, however, that certain conditions of labor can so affect the person, ruining his health, destroying his morale, darkening his mind, that equivalently, we are using the person and not merely his work. In between, of course, there is a grey area where it is not always clear whether the person or his work is being used.

These observations force us to make a rough division of spheres of importance in man. Starting from the highest level, the person as a person, we descend to his intellect and will, his body and then his external activity. At the same time we recognize that in the concrete, harm to the body can often be equivalent to an attack on the higher spheres. We must always examine the total effects on a person in all his spheres, lest we use a rough distinction to justify activity which is truly harmful.

The fact that man is a totality existing in time has further important implications for ethics. Abstractly, everything should be ordered to the higher faculties and ultimately to the person. But in practice we are often forced to postpone the development of higher powers to tend to immediate and urgent demands of a lower sort. Thus, food, shelter and clothing must be had here and now lest the whole man die, while education can often be put off for a time without any final harm to the individual. The importance of this simple idea will appear in the chapter on business and waste.

The division of spheres of importance in man also has significance for a man's role as a member of society or an employee of a firm. Granted that man as a whole should never be used as a means to anything except the perfection of the individual himself, a person may, and often must, subordinate his activity to the good of others either individually or in groups. Such a subordination of lesser goods (time, comfort, security, recreation) is necessary for social cooperation, which in its turn is necessary for the good of individuals.

These seemingly abstract statements are of great importance in business, for the employee, while retaining his dignity and inalienable rights as a man, is, as a worker, subject to the good of the firm and of those who depend on the firm. This subordination has limits, but it exists. Thus, a manager cannot impose serious burdens on the worker in order to obtain some minor benefit for the enterprise. On the other hand, he can and sometimes must, fire or demote a man for the good of others.

The application of these principles can often be difficult, for a manager cannot always be sure at what point the sacrifice of the lesser goods may reduce man to the level of a thing, or at what point the potential harm to others would be greater than the potential gain to an individual. To make such judgments requires a grasp of the facts and only the manager himself can obtain these.

None of this should cause the businessman or anyone else to forget that man is a free and responsible agent. Paternalism may be the correct approach to a child, it is an insult to an adult and an unnecessary burden to one in authority. It is not always kind to protect a person from the consequences of his own stupidity. It can often be stultifying to give what a person has not earned. An executive should not attempt to be a father to his workers.

Freedom has another important implication for business. Loyalty and cooperation cannot be bought. Yet the success of most enterprises depends in large part on just these qualities. For business reasons, then, if not for ethical ones, the manager should remember that he must respect the dignity of his employees if he is to have them as efficient members of his team. The chapters on psychological testing and decision by computer will consider some areas where the executive must be on his guard against violating the rights of his employees, and losing their loyalty.

The previous remarks presuppose that the employer, though he must respect the dignity of those with whom he deals directly, also has an obligation to the interests of the firm and to the groups which depend on it. The executive is charged with taking care of a sort of common weal. He must consider the effects his acts will have on all involved. To do so correctly, he must enlarge his notion of the good of business and the firm.

Business

Writers such as Peter Drucker and Richard Eells have begun
exploring the meaning of modern business.[3] Their works should
be read by anyone seriously interested in attacking ethical problems in this field. There is room here only to underline certain
facets of modern business which have a peculiar effect on ethical
decisions.

The word business can stand for a firm, the entire business
community, or the process by which goods are manufactured and
distributed. In all three senses of the word, business exists to
satisfy the economic needs of men. Neither the firm, nor the
community, nor the process, is an end. Though all three are
means, they have a peculiar necessity and nature. A business is
a human society in which men work together to satisfy their own
needs by satisfying the needs of others. The necessity of cooperation gives the firm a position of importance both as a social tool
and as a means to the perfection of its employees. The cooperation, as already noted, cannot be bought, it is to be created and
fostered. As a result, a concern for this truly human aspect of
business is a prime obligation of the manager.

In the days before organized labor was a real force, the manager sometimes forgot that human relations were possibly more
decisive than technical efficiency. So too, there was a day when
many did not see that the attitudes of workers were more important for productivity than the mechanical organization of
work. Today, however, it is clear that the long-range good of
an enterprise may often demand that technical considerations be
sacrificed, to maintain the efficiency of the human factor. This
important conclusion implies that an enlarged view of a firm's requirements will often show that even lesser goods of the worker
should not be subordinated to some mechanical rule of thumb.
Thus, where a purely scientific cost analysis might demand layoffs, a broader view might indicate that these layoffs would hurt

the company in the long-run. To put it another way, increased appreciation of the true nature of business can reduce the area in which a manager might feel an ethical strain.

In making decisions which will influence workers, whether manual, white collar or managerial, the executive must remember that their reaction depends on their expectations, implicit as well as contractual. Thus, the modern worker expects that dismissals will follow some form of due procedure. Further, even though a company does not guarantee a job formally, there may be an expectation that it will protect seniority. A violation of such assumptions may lead to serious harm, even though the executive may think that he is being fair. For this reason, and despite the complexities introduced by unions, the manager must be very sensitive to the human atmosphere he functions in.

Since an individual firm is not only a society but part of a business community, relating with suppliers, dealers and consumers, a truly comprehensive view would demand that the manager consider not only the rights, but the reactions and expectations of these groups as well. Indeed, unless managers give more consideration to these relationships, there is a possibility that additional legislation will be forthcoming.[4] If nothing else, the businessman should remember that self-interest is not really enlightened unless it is large enough to identify itself, at least in part, with the interests of others.[5] Management's obligation to a firm implies a duty to consider carefully the interests of all who are involved in its affairs.

Though short-sightedness and greed can sometimes obscure these facts from businessmen, perhaps the biggest obstacle to seeing them is a reliance on the excuses furnished by the classical business creed. According to this, the manager was both a victim and an agent of impersonal market forces. His job was to adapt to them and seek a short-range maximization of profit. If he dared to look at larger issues, he could expect failure, or at least seriously reduced profits. This type of theory reduced the

responsibilities of business leaders and excused them from
making many difficult decisions.

Today, such a theory is no longer universally applicable—if
indeed it ever was. Large corporations in particular are often
insulated from the full impact of market forces. Peter Drucker
believes the whole theory is badly founded.

Economic forces set limits to what management can do. They create
opportunities for management's action. But they, by themselves, do
not determine what a business is, or what it does. Nothing could be
sillier than the oft-repeated assertion that "management only adapts
the business to the forces of the market." Management not only finds
these "forces"; management creates them by its own actions.[6]

All this implies that management has a positive creative
function. A firm "does not merely adjust to the market, it helps
to create it." It does not accept the *status quo*, but attempts to
change it in such a way as to satisfy the demands of stockholders,
suppliers, dealers, workers and the general public. If management refuses to accept this and continues to appeal to the theory
of impersonal market forces, it will create situations which will
call for legislation. At present, indeed, there is need for creative
action to stabilize production and employment, to provide for
workers idled by automation and to develop new markets which
will provide for the future health of the economy. This in turn
brings up the question of business and the larger society.

Business and the Larger Society

A firm exists in a larger society of which it is only a part and
a servant. Even though the enterprise may be private in the
sense of not being an organ of the state, it has a social function.
No one will really quibble about this, but there is dispute as to

how this function is fulfilled and who is responsible for fulfilling it.

In a classic theory based on the assumption of perfect competition, a firm either satisfied the demands of society or went out of business. Theoretically in a world of numerous small businesses, no one firm was in a position either to beat the law of competition or to exercise a decisive impact on either the economy or society as a whole. In such a world, there was assumed to be a harmony of interests which worked out automatically. It would have been useless and even blasphemous for a manager to have tried to serve the public in any way but by energetic competition.

This may still be true for the small or medium-sized business. However, the appearance of the giant corporation, and of imperfect, not to say semi-monopolistic, competition has changed that for many firms. Even though it is not possible to give an exact evaluation of the power of these corporations, it is clear that they do have more freedom and more impact on society than did the small family owned and managed business of classical theory. General Motors' decision to invest a billion dollars in expansion is credited with having averted one recession. Settlements about wages in steel and the automotive industries certainly affect wage and price levels in the whole economy. A strike in a key industry such as trucking could paralyze the entire nation.

To the extent that they have such power, managers cannot assume that what is good for their company is automatically in the best interests of the nation. On the contrary, the good of the enterprise is tied up with its willingness to respect the good of the economy and the society as a whole. Society cannot leave such power in private hands unless it is used for the public weal. To do so would be to disregard its own responsibilities. On the other hand, government regulation is the least desirable form of social control, for political as well as economic reasons.

It is for this reason that Peter Drucker rightly insists that management of the large corporation has a responsibility "to consider such demands as made by society (or likely to be made in the near future) as may affect the attainment of the business objectives of the enterprise."[7] Indeed, since small businesses in their totality may have an even greater effect on public opinion and policy, the business community as a whole has a collective responsibility to be sensitive to the demands of society.

As Drucker has so forcibly pointed out, this public responsibility is bound up with responsibility to the firm and its workers. All three, for example, will benefit if the large corporations can develop a capital expenditure policy which will counteract the extremes of business cycles. All three will profit, if business in conjunction with government and the unions can work out policies which will stabilize incomes. All three will profit if we can work out solutions to the problem of the older worker, and those displaced by technological advance. All three will also lose if business fails to meet these responsibilities. When government steps in, business will lose much of even its legitimate freedom, the public will lose one countervailing force, and the workers will find that they too have lost independence when they must deal with the government rather than with another private group.

Business and management may not want these responsibilities. They may argue that they should not have them. But, like it or not, the situation has created the responsibilities, and business must accept them, or pay the penalty.

We must recognize that not all companies have the same power, so that not all managers have the same obligation to consider the demands of society as a whole. Power, moreover, is not an absolute but a relative attribute of a company, so that even smaller firms may have some of these obligations with regard to local communities in which they are a major employer. In addition, power is not all inclusive, even in the largest companies. They may be powerful in one realm of business and not in another. The responsibility which follows power will also be limited to particular realms. These distinctions are important, for they should prevent the businessman from thinking that ethics makes him responsible for the whole of the public weal in every area of the country.

The distinctions are important too, because they indicate that responsibilities cannot be assigned until factual investigation has shown where and to what extent individual industries and companies have power over areas of grave importance to the public good. The chapter on business power and public opinion will study one of these areas.

Even though these distinctions may limit the area of public responsibility, there remains the very difficult problem of discharging these duties when they do exist. Often the holders of corporate power in one area cannot discharge their obligation without inviting retaliation in another. Thus, though a company may have the power to hold the line on prices in order to slow inflation, attempts to do so will often be attacked by the unions, which may feel that the policy sacrifices the desires of workers for pay increases. This means that in practice, the manager cannot fulfill a duty without the cooperation of the unions. If labor and management do cooperate, they must face the possibility that they will arouse cries of private conspiracy. Indeed, the very cooperation of labor in management which is necessary for the public weal might bring into existence a power which is potentially very dangerous to society as a whole.

These possibilities indicate that even a broadening of managerial outlook and a recognition of public responsibilities will not solve the problem of power. In some way we need to develop new institutional frameworks which enable the managers of big corporations to fulfill responsibilities without running the risk of severe retaliation from power holders in other sectors. If this is to be done without increasing state intervention, business leaders must accept as a basic responsibility the need to escape the molds of the status quo and to rethink the possibilities.

Some, of course, would solve the problem of power merely by creating countervailing powers. This policy, if successful, may limit power and the dangers that flow from it, but it does not guarantee that power will be used correctly. The prevention of abuse is not equivalent to the promotion of correct use. Further, when the countervailing powers are few in number, the balance is always precarious and can break down easily, unless maintained by some force outside the system. At its worst, the theory of countervailing power is merely the old classical theory of competition transferred to a market in which only a few have real power. Like the old classical creed, it suffers from the assumption that some invisible hand will bring the social optimum out of conflict. American society has already realized that countervailing power cannot settle all problems automatically. The use of injunctions in strikes which threaten the public health and welfare is one example where special legislation has come into being because a deadlock led to abuses.

We are left, then, with many questions of power undecided. Once again, the prime obligation on business is to devote itself to a serious study of its relation to the larger society. Unfortunately, this obligation has often been neglected, for business, so proud of its flexibility and rationality in the technical fields, is liable to be over-conservative and anti-intellectual.[8] As a result, business often uses outmoded slogans at a time when real thought is needed for the good of society and business itself. All this means that progress will depend on the businessman's ability to free himself from the prejudices which are born of the ethos and the American business creed.

Conclusions

Despite the large number of unsolved problems, certain basic conclusions can be drawn from these brief considerations of man, business and society. In later chapters on business and waste, and business and public opinion, we shall attempt to work through some of the concrete implications of these positions.

Business exists for man and not man for business. The person as a person is never to be used as a means. At the same time, because business is necessary for men and society, the work of individuals must be subject to the good of the firm. In practice, many problems can be avoided if it is remembered that what wins the loyalty of employers, customers, suppliers and dealers, is in the long-run also to the best interest of the firm.

In general, it is not the function of a firm to work *directly* for the promotion of all aspects of the public weal. While it must see that its activity is conformable to the public good, its direct and primary obligation is care for the particular goods of those involved in the company. On the whole, the good of society is best served when the company strives to produce useful goods at the lowest possible cost and to sell them at the lowest price consistent with fair wages, with a fair return on investment and with the long-range health of the company. In short, the primary obligation of the businessman is to run his business as well as possible.

What must be eliminated are false ideas about what constitutes good business itself. Profit is not a sign of success if it has been earned at the expense of either the public, the workers or the stockholders. Nor is profit a criterion when it has resulted not from providing a real economic service, but from the use of power, fraud or trickery. However, granted correct notions about business, our general principle holds true in most cases.

Exceptions seem to arise when a business has a unique position in the economy or is subject to abnormal influences. For instance, a public utility which supplies an absolutely necessary product may be obliged to continue serving the public even when it is not profitable to do so. Again, a corporation so large as to have a decisive influence on the local or the national economy may be obliged to sacrifice the temporary interests of stockholders in order to avoid severe harm to the economy. Even these, however, are not real exceptions to our principle, for if the company fails to serve the public in these cases, it runs the risk of subjecting itself to government regulations and even to extinction. This is merely to say that public service is often good business, at least in twentieth century America.

In the following chapters we shall treat certain obligations to society, to workers and to industry in detail. Here, we wish only to stress that business responsibilities are complex and best met by improving the quality of business itself. Yet, there is something fundamental behind this simple thesis. The complexity of the problem, both in the ethical and the technical sphere, indicates that there can be no solution unless the businessman attacks his work not only with high ideals, but with a creative competence which can find the way to implement the demands of conscience and to realize its ideals.

Notes

1. *Cf.* Francis X. Sutton, Seymour E. Harris, Carl Kaysen, James Tobin, *The American Business Creed* (Harvard University Press, 1956), p. 341.
2. *Cf.* Jean Mouroux, *The Meaning of Man* (Image Books, 1961) and Joseph Wood Krutch, *The Measure of Man* (Bobbs-Merrill, 1954).
3. Anyone seriously interested in these questions should read Peter F. Drucker, *Concept of the Corporation* (John Day, 1946); *The New Society* (Harper and Brothers, 1949), and *The Practice of Management* (Harper and Brothers, 1954) and Richard Eells, *The Meaning of Modern Business* (Columbia University Press, 1960).
4. Several of the essays in Edward S. Mason (ed.), *The Corporation in Modern Society* (Harvard University Press, 1959), touch on this point. *Cf.* pp. 43-44; 77; 98; 234-236.

5. *Cf.* John Maurice Clark, *Economic Institutions and Human Welfare* (Knopf, 1957), p. 207.
6. *The Practice of Management*, p. 34.
7. *Ibid.*, p. 385.
8. Sutton, *et al.*, *op. cit.*, pp. 381-382.

Readings

Richard Eells and Clarence Walton, *Conceptual Foundations of Modern Business* (Irwin, 1961); Kenneth Boulding, *The Organizational Revolution* (Harper and Brothers, 1953); John Maurice Clark, *Social Control of Business* (University of Chicago, 1926).

Marquis W. Childs and Douglas Cater, *Ethics in a Business Society* (Harper and Brothers, 1954).

Clarence B. Randall, *A Creed for Free Enterprise* (Little, Brown and Company, 1952).

Benjamin M. Selekman, *A Moral Philosophy for Management* (McGraw-Hill, 1959).

Sylvia K. and Benjamin M. Selekman, *Power and Morality in a Business Society* (McGraw-Hill, 1956).

W. Lloyd Warner and Norman H. Martin (eds.), *Industrial Man: Businessmen and Business Organizations* (Harper and Brothers, 1959).

Theodore W. Schultz, "Investment in Human Capital," *The American Economic Review*, March, 1961 (vol. 51, no. 1), pp. 1-17; Robert N. Anthony, "The Trouble with Profit Maximization," *Harvard Business Review*, November-December, 1960 (vol. 38, no. 6), pp. 125-134.

4 WORK

THOUGH BUSINESS ETHICS tends to be concerned with specific practices and situations, the personal moral problems of the businessman are often centered on work itself. Many suffer from a feeling that they are wasting their lives selling chewing gum, writing press releases, or designing bigger and better bowling alleys. Even when there is no feeling of real guilt, the businessman often carries a burden of meaninglessness about with him. Unfortunately the meaning one finds in work, and the attitude towards it, have much to do not only with the direction of one's life, but also with the way one handles specific ethical problems. Ultimately, a man's personal philosophy of work will have a great deal to do with his approach to business ethics. In the modern context, a man's ideas about work are decisive in creating that ethos which will penetrate, modify and color all his business decisions.

The Ideal

Once upon a time, in the not-too-long-ago, work was looked on as a commodity. Labor was bought and sold like wheat or jute or machine tools. Both in theory and fact its value was largely determined by what you could buy with it. Work in such an ethos was hardly a human thing, and indeed, the conditions of toil were such that they tended to make men into animals. Even though this idea was applied principally to the laboring man, the businessman and the manager suffered from its application. At the very least, the commodity theory of labor caused the entrepreneur to evaluate his efforts in terms of the market rather than within a broader human context.

Since Marx, who so violently flayed the commodity theory of work, we have had to cope with another extreme position. For Marx, work was not one activity among others, it was the specifically human activity which almost by itself was to achieve the human good. This is not surprising, for if the good of man is to be measured only by his material well-being, work is certainly the privileged instrument of its attainment. Though Americans hardly subscribe to the pure Marxist doctrine of work, all those who accept the end of man as identical with his material well-being tend to see work as the unique means to this end. A distorted idea of human life necessarily leads to a distorted idea of work itself.

The American business creed, which tends to judge success at work in terms of salary and profitability, has only served to confuse the issue further. Such a standard blurs the meaning of work, for according to it, producing cigarettes is as important as growing food. Love of quality and workmanship are subordinated to profitability. This tends to rob work of even such meaning as it may have as an expression of human creativity.

The Christian concept of work stands in opposition[1] to both Marx and the classical economists. The concept, at once complex and rich in historical development, follows from the Christian concept of man and of his relations to God and the world.[2] At times the concept has suffered serious damage from heretical distortions, but in its main outlines, it continues to flourish even while struggling to relate itself to the conditions of modern work.

Work for the Christian is first of all, says Cardinal Lecaro,[3] a human activity, not a commodity, not a product, much less a unique vocation or a supreme glory to which all ought to be sacrificed. As an activity of man, work has its part to play in the development of man. This would have been true even if Adam had not fallen, for work is a creative and not a penal activity. At the same time, it follows that work, even hard work, has value. It is not something to be despised as beneath the dignity of a gentleman, or something to be avoided as an obstacle to holiness. Yet, being only a part, work can never become either a final end or the unique means of human perfection.

Once put into this setting, work begins to emerge as something deeper than a mere means of earning a living, though, of course, this remains a prime purpose. In the first place, work appears as the artistic, creative drive by which man transforms the world and society into an instrument of human perfection. Like all human operations, it is also a collaboration with the Creator in His labor to provide for man. Granted that work is not always this, this is what it ought to be.

In our age where work is almost essentially social, performed with, and for the benefit of, other men, it can and should be an expression of love. Indeed, often it is the only expression for the thousands and the millions whom we never see and will never know. Work transforms the world and renders it a more fitting place for others to dwell in. Viewed on a cosmic scale, the worker is like the father who furnishes a home so that those he loves may have a center of life in which to develop. As we shall see in the next sections, work often falls short of this, but the ideal remains.

When work realizes the ideal of creativity and love, it almost necessarily involves sacrifice, toil, and even boredom. The reason is simple. While work may be natural to man, the conditions under which he works are still a consequence of the fall of Adam. In this it is like nearly all human activity. It must carry the burden of frailty and face the obstacles set up by sin. Despite this, indeed because of this, work has a place in the redemption of mankind, so long as the sacrifice and toil are viewed as a price paid to restore the world to the harmony desired by God. Indeed, insofar as man does restore this harmony, his work becomes a note in a hymn of praise offered to God.

The Reality

Though the Christian ideals retain their validity, their beauty and their appeal, no one can deny that the prevalent meaning of work is far removed from them. We have eliminated much of the harshness connected with physical labor, but we have not succeeded in giving work the full human and divine significance which it ought to have. Interviews with businessmen and white collar workers unearth a profound discontent, a frustration, a feeling of guilt connected with their work. For many their labor is meaningless except as a means of life. For others their work is a betrayal of youthful ideals, or a drudgery that must be suffered. Strangely enough this dissatisfaction seems almost more common in the business and white collar class than among manual laborers and craftsmen. What is wrong? How does one transpose the ideal into the real order?

Neither of these questions can be answered unless we understand something of the nature of modern work, and of the human conditions which surround it. Without such understanding any effort to reconcile ideal and real will end up in a sort of poetry, beautiful but neither true nor helpful, except as material for day-dreams.

Perhaps the most striking thing about much of the work men must do to earn a living is that it actually *is* often meaningless or close to meaningless. It is difficult to convince oneself that there is any great cosmic significance in advertising cosmetics, selling toy balloons or peddling whiskey. This is especially so when one is aware that these involve the use of time, energy, skill and material that would be better used elsewhere, if only it were "economically" feasible. Even when this is not consciously felt, it remains active on the subconscious level.

The sense of meaninglessness, however, is not confined to work which produces exchange value but little social utility. It crops up even in areas where the worker is performing a real service. Thus, salesmen of insurance often feel guilty, not because insurance is useless, but because they see themselves selling more than people can afford to buy. At the same time they are constantly aware of the time and energy wasted in competition which is not real competition, and in endless running around. Advertising men and salesmen in general seem prey to the same sort of moral uneasiness, not because they violate clear moral principles, but because they sense the futility of what they are doing.

This situation is not, of course, merely the result of the conditions of work. It springs from the very nature of demand in modern economies. We produce what people want and can pay for. If they want useless things before they have satisfied real needs, they will get them and so others will be forced to supply them or find themselves without even a livelihood. In short, the meaninglessness of much work results from the meaninglessness of the demand and the futility of the desires which bring it about. To put it yet another way, the individual finds himself uneasy, because, like it or not, he is working in the service of pagan values. The social philosophy of production and consumption, then, has a great deal to do with the meaning of work; the Christian ideal of work cannot be realized without a reform of the existing ideal of human life in the economic sphere. Till this millennium is reached, millions are doomed to some degree of frustration.

The secularist does not feel this tension to the same extent as the Christian. He can and does, though not always with complete success, kid himself that so long as he satisfies desires, his own and other people's, provides jobs and keeps the economy moving, he has done his duty. Behind this lies the idea that what is produced does not matter so long as it is profitable, and acceptable to society. Even farther behind this is the conviction that life itself is rather meaningless.

Even work which is truly useful and ultimately has meaning may not appear so to the worker because, in modern economies, both the workman and the white collar worker are too far removed from the end product to realize its significance. Despite the changes in economic organization, men are still suffering from the alienation of which Marx spoke so eloquently. One does not have to be a Communist to see that the day of craftsmanship is gone and that men are more than ever robbed of satisfaction in their work. Indeed, with the increasing systemization and division of labor even in business and the white collar professions, this alienation is liable to grow rather than diminish. Neither the bookkeeper in his cell, nor the media expert in the advertising agency, nor the buyer in a big department store is free of this division between himself and the product of his labor. Even teachers may not escape, if the teaching machine and the standardized test and the audiovisual aid separate him from his pupils.

The incidental features of this situation only exacerbate the feeling of frustration. The division of labor which increases productivity also forces many to work below their capacity,[4] and the real talents either rust in man unused or are turned to leisure activity. Each year sees well-endowed college graduates going forth to a life of routine detail; the growth of do-it-yourself indicates not only economic need, but a need to put one's personal imprint on something, and to expand the unused capacities.

There is no easy solution to this problem. Without a division and rationalization of work, our civilization would collapse. Perhaps the whole thing has been overdone, but perhaps too there is need for a rethinking of the relation between work and leisure, and a reorientation of the worker, which will enable him to see beyond the confines of his own office or cubicle.

Actually much that is meaningless is also unnecessary. There are methods of organization which, while compatible with mass production, do not lead to boredom, isolation and meaninglessness. Indeed, it would almost seem as if those methods are more efficient because they lead to a better and more human use of human resource.[5]

The meaninglessness and alienation present in so much white-collar work are perhaps less dangerous than the demands which work puts not on a man's time and talent, but on his personality. The managers, of course, are conscious that meaninglessness and alienation are the enemies of productivity and profit. As a result they have attempted to find surrogates for what we might call the natural satisfactions. Unfortunately, these substitutes are liable to increase the problem for the worker. At the risk of seeming cynical, we must examine some of these ersatz satisfactions and their consequences.

Precisely because the relationship between the individual and the fruit of his work is barely discernible, the management must put the stress on the group.[6] This, to a certain extent, fits in with the preoccupation of the manager for whom the company may come to be a value in itself. In any event, one or more of these tendencies lead to an effort to build up company loyalty, and to an extreme stress on the quality of interpersonal relationships. These emphases, in their turn, produce further problems, for the individual if not for the company.

The company loyalty program with its "big happy family" theme can almost amount to a sort of "My company right or wrong" attitude. I have on occasion even met so fantastic a loyalty, that I thought I was talking to a member of a religious order rather than to a middle executive in a major American industrial firm. Such loyalty can, by making a man feel part of something bigger, attenuate the effects of the meaninglessness of his actual job. At the same time it does not really solve the problem itself unless the job gives scope for the use of personal judgment. More important, however, is the fact that it involves a loyalty which hardly seems due to an anonymous corporation. Indeed, the existence of such an atmosphere may even make work more difficult for the man who wants to possess his own soul.

In extreme cases where loyalty to the company involves one's family, home, recreation, style of dress and tone of life, this substitute for job satisfaction may tend to swallow up the rest of life. It is almost as if work was in fact, if not in theory, *the* activity in life; though here, as opposed to the Communist state, the work is work for a particular private economic entity.[7] This picture is exaggerated: the seeds have been planted, but the flower has not appeared as yet. However, the very possibility of it shows that loyalty to the group is not a panacea for the problems of bureaucracy.

In the last analysis the group loyalty approach spills over into the personality approach. In modern business where the ability to manipulate people is *a* prime, if not *the* prime, managerial skill, personality is all important, at least below the highest level of command. The man who wants to get ahead must tailor his personality to the role he desires. If he is already involved in the ethos of loyalty, this amounts to instrumentalizing, not merely his work, but his being. As Mills has expressed it, the rise of personality markets has carried self and social alienation to explicit extremes.[8] Herzberg even feels that in cases where hiring and advancement depend on personality rather than skill, the individual may learn to avoid too great a display of technical skill.[9]

While discussion and analysis of the meaninglessness of work might be carried on endlessly, these few remarks will serve to indicate why it is difficult to realize the Christian ideal of work in the present order of things. It also indicates that the problem is not superficial but one which involves deep strata of man's being.

False Solutions

In the face of this problem modern men, including many religious men, have tried two false solutions. The first we shall call cenobitic withdrawal; the second, surrender. These solutions, of course, parallel the basic intellectual positions regarding the material world found in the so-called eschatologist and incarnationist schools of human culture. Here we shall not concern ourselves with the deeper roots.

The would-be cenobite is filled with nostalgia for a simpler world where the crafts were supreme and the family not only the primary, but almost the final, social unity. What we may call the extreme fringe, the utopists, have actually tried to realize this world. As a mass solution it is all too clearly chimerical.

The majority take a different approach. They accept the fact that their work is often meaningless, and raise higher the wall between work and life: wandering off to seek meaning elsewhere. Work is a necessary evil and families, hobbies or friends become the whole of life. Work is at best a sacrifice of time necessary to build a life outside work.[10]

This, of course, does not solve the problem. It isolates it and denies it, without enriching either the individual or his life. It is a supine solution and all of a piece with the lack of responsibility of which we have already spoken. For the Christian it is worse than no solution, for it implies a refusal to change the world, and often involves a real indifference to the moral and social impact of work.

Casual observation indicates that many have taken this path. They are content with a job which gives them a decent income; content with a position which does not involve too much responsibility; content to leave the great problems to others. The prevalence of this attitude is not comforting when one considers the power which belongs to those who reach the top.

The man who runs away from his work and from the problems it poses, is liable to be the man who does not participate in professional associations, since this would involve him; he is liable to be the man who avoids the social implications of his work; he is certainly not the man who will create a better world or solve real ethical problems. For this reason, the solution of cenobitic withdrawal must be rejected.

The other solution, the solution of surrender, is equally objectionable, and from a moral point of view possibly even more dangerous. Here there is a full dedication to work but the goal is no longer to transform the world, or to find meaning in work. Income, status and power are the goals. Again, the problem is by-passed rather than solved.

Now, though one cannot condemn either income, status or power as motives for work, they are dangerous motives, for they can distort not only the economy as a whole but the very personality of the worker. The danger is especially great when they are promoted to the rank of final goals, for then they may swallow up the rest of life, distort basic values and add to the meaninglessness of the work itself.

Such an approach cuts work off from higher values, isolates it from life and does away with real ethical standards. Other men tend to become means to one's personal goals. In this perspective it is meaningless to talk of duties even to the enterprise, let alone to society as a whole.

At the same time, the man of good-will cannot as a rule transform the business world without power, status and income. These are, and always will be, important tools. Anyone who despises them is living apart from the mainstream of modern life; only those who control these three forces will be able to change the business world and the conditions of work. Thus, insofar as the Christian businessman has an obligation to change the world, he has an obligation to seek those means which are necessary and legitimate tools for the attainment of the end. He must not, however, confuse the means with the end, nor allow himself to be devoured by the desire for them.

One point needs to be emphasized in this context. Often the

drive for success is an escape from more mature responsibility, and at times it almost seems that success in business demands so wholehearted a dedication to the "bitch Goddess" that a Christian cannot both save his soul and gain that position necessary to change the world. This brings us to a consideration of the factors that must be weighed before the individual can take a valid position with regard to work.

Other Dimensions of the Problem

From what has been said up to now, it should be clear that the ideal of work is not something that can be realized by a few mental adjustments. It is an ideal, and its realization demands that men work to change not merely institutional structures, but the value system of society as a whole. In addition, it is evident that this cannot be achieved unless the businessman is fully aware of his obligations, both social and individual, as well as of his own capacities and limitations. To put it yet another way, there is an obligation to think out the problem: but in order to do so, it is necessary to establish a real discipline in one's own personal life. It is an immense task, which entails re-evaluating all the other spheres in which one lives.

In the first place, the businessman has to take a stand with regard to his own family. The number of guilt complexes connected with neglecting the family show that this is a real problem. It is almost a commonplace today that those who set up a comfortable nest in the suburbs find themselves cut off from the very family they are trying to build. The commuter who sees his children for a few minutes at dawn and dusk; the salesman who is forever on the road; the executive whose week-ends are eroded by business-social engagements; the couples who are forced to deal socially with business associates they do not like, are all faced with the same problem. At times, of course, not merely home life, but health and sanity are at stake. The problem is essentially one of choiçe. What norm is a man to follow?

To make things even more confusing, the conflicting demands of family and business are mixed in with the demands of the community and the church and the neighborhood. The PTA, local politics, charitable drives, church affairs, all have some claim on a man's time, but time and energy are so limited. Choice is imperative, but on what principles?

Many in our society avoid choice. They drift and hope that events or higher-ups or whim will solve the problem. But, to repeat, this merely bypasses the problem; it does not even touch on a real solution.

Some Principles

The actual conditions of work indicate that modern man is torn between the danger of losing his soul in work and the danger of losing it by a refusal to work. Worse yet, the possibility of finding a middle course is complicated by the meaninglessness of much work and by the dehumanizing atmosphere around him. While some few can solve their individual problem by picking the right job, this option is not open to most. Indeed, society would suffer if all men, or even a large group of them, shunned the routine work which is still a necessity. So difficult is the situation, that even those who do not reject the true ideal of work, reconcile themselves to the status quo and seek to find themselves and their salvation in other spheres of life.

The first obligation is to form a correct idea of work. The second is to embrace the ideal as a personal and social goal, however difficult of attainment. Unless the ideal is seen as something to be done, the field will be left open to those who would turn society and work into instruments of a purely secular ideal, leaving no place for the true development of the individual. If the ideal is treated as only a dream, it and the values which surround it will erode until the rest of man's inner life suffers. In short, a tactic of isolation and defense will not work.

A realistic appraisal of the situation indicates the need for a three-sided attack. First, the atmosphere of work and the values of others must be changed. Second, the conditions of work must be changed. Third, the use of leisure must be cultivated so as to harmonize with the need for true human development.

Since the situation is the work of a whole series of causes and conditions, no one man can hope to cope with it. To protect his own ideals and realize his duties, he must have allies. Now, since much of the difficulty resides in a demand for goods that are meaningless and in a theory of work that is not Christian, these must be changed before anything else can be done. Obviously, this is the work of a lifetime, but so are all great works. It is, moreover, the basic task. As one top ranking executive put it to me, "My job is to educate the thousands of people who have it in their power to make decisions. Until that is done, no codes are going to mean very much."

This change is not going to be made by mere preaching, nor even by good example. Granted the pragmatic outlook of many businessmen, indeed of many Americans, it is necessary to show them that their present activities and attitudes are actually destructive of their own ideals, limited though these ideals be. This demonstration, of course, requires information, study, thought, and the ability to speak a language which is intelligible to business associates.

People being what they are, a purely negative approach will not suffice to transform the world of work. The natural reaction to criticism is "Show me a better way." This means that the Christian must have workable alternatives to the present way of doing things. He must have not only an ideal, but clear and practical ways of putting it into practice. This means an obligation to be in the forefront of technological progress, sensitive to both its dangers and its possibilities, open to advances and creative thinking in industrial relations, human relations, engineering, psychology, management planning and personnel work.

Those aware of the possibilities and dangers of automation can intuit the need for men who are both technically competent and properly oriented. Automation contains the seeds of a real revolution which will change the meaning of work once again. For some it will mean the possibility of controlling and guiding rather than merely tending machines. It will create the need for new professions and for expert knowledge. It may upgrade labor and put a premium on truly human characteristics. At the same time, if not properly used it can increase tensions, make men slaves of machines and turn the factory and the office into great antiseptic halls patrolled by lonely human beings. Here is a real challenge in the world of work.

Leisure and Work

Even granted that long slow labor can transform the nature of work, it remains true that technological and social change will continue to alter the balance between work and leisure. Leisure will almost undoubtedly come to occupy a great portion of our day, and an increasingly important part of our life. Indeed, leisure itself will be transformed from periods used to recreate us for work, into periods when a man does his real work. Leisure, which often tends to be swallowed up in mere entertainment or relaxation, can, of course, be devoted to improving our minds and spirits. It gives opportunity for prayer and self-expression and social life.

I suspect, however, that if the world is to be transformed we must also have time for all that work which, while it has little market value, is of the utmost importance to the individual and society. The new leisure can provide parents with a chance to take over some of the formal education of their children, and provide opportunity for political participation and community work. At the same time, it could give rise to new activity in professional organizations and, through this, to the development of a better ethos for the work one does for a living. To put it another way, the ideal of work, that is, of the creative transformation of the world by human toil, may find its real locus in the time we now call leisure, the time that is economically not productive. Indeed, we might even arrive at a point where earning a living is looked on as activity that distracts us from our real work in the world.

This suggestion may seem farfetched, not only because mass leisure has never been extensive enough to admit of such a possibility, but because the new propaganda presents leisure as a time for consumption of products and for pleasure as an end in itself. The idea seems to be to treat the time left over from formal work (i.e. income earning) as a sort of vacuum which must be filled with distraction, gadgets, and the adaptation of the pursuits of what is supposed to be a cultural elite. From an ethical point of view such promotion of leisure is not without its dangers, the greatest of which is that it may distract from the possibilities of using this time for truly creative work of a social sort.

Strangely enough, it is the managerial men who are tending to spend a good part of their leisure in home duties, volunteer associations and church work. At the same time blue- and white-collar males seem to favor radio, T.V., the movies, and sports. This means that just those who are least liable to have found real satisfaction in their wage-earning work are most liable to have an escapist form of leisure time activity.

The full implications of leisure and its use would carry us far beyond the scope of this chapter. Yet the movement of the times indicates that the problem of wage earning work is only one phase of the larger and growing problem of work and leisure time in American life. What is suggested here is the possibility of using the new leisure time to explore the larger meaning and significance of business, the economy and the society. Indeed, it may be providential that we will have more time for this, at the very moment when such rethinking has become imperative.

In reorganizing our conceptual scheme, we must beware of certain aberrations. In the first place, though non-income-earning toil may increase as an important part of life, and indeed enable man to restore real meaning to his work, much income-earning labor will retain its importance for society. The market economy is of great importance and cannot be neglected without serious harm. Starry-eyed idealism must be tempered by hard-headed practicality, which sees that ideals are often attainable only in terms of existing institutional structures.

Summary

Work must be seen as a truly creative human task, which, while providing for the needs of the worker, should also be a contribution to the real welfare of other men. The needs of the worker include not only income, but creativity and participation in a society broader than the family. At the same time, work cannot be *the* activity of man for he has other needs of equal and greater importance. Although man has an obligation to work, he must not surrender himself to it completely.

This balance of attitude is necessary if the worker, and especially the manager, is to succeed in realizing himself as a man. Moreover, it is a necessary perspective if they are to see their obligation to transform the world of work so that it more efficiently serves both the worker and society.

Notes

1. C. Wright Mills, *White Collar* (Oxford University Press, Galaxy Edition, 1956), p. 216, concentrates on Protestant interpretations of work. Sebastian De Grazia, *Of Time, Work and Leisure* (Twentieth Century Fund, 1962), *passim* has many interesting remarks on the question, but they appear to be a bit one-sided.
2. *Cf.* Robert W. Gleason, S.J., *Christ and the Christian* (Sheed and Ward, 1959), pp. 147-171; H. Rondet, "A Theology of Work," *Theology Digest,* Winter, 1956 (vol. 4), pp. 37-42. John M. Todd (ed.), *Work: Christian Thought and Practice* (Baltimore: Helicon Press, 1960).
3. Here and in the following pages I have followed Cardinal Giacomo Lecaro's address to the Instituto Superiori di Cultura Religiosa of the Gregorian University, Rome, in April of 1961.
4. Mills, *op. cit.,* p. 224.
5. Frederick Herzberg, Bernard Mausner and Barbara Bloch Snyderman, *The Motivation to Work* (John Wiley and Sons, 1959), p. 129.
6. Mills, *op. cit.,* p. 225.
7. *Cf.* Herzberg, *op. cit.,* pp. 120-139.
8. Mills, *op. cit.,* p. 228.
9. Herzberg, *op. cit.,* p. 129.
10. *Cf.* De Grazia, *op. cit.,* chapter IV.

Readings

The Editors of Fortune, *The Executive Life* (Doubleday, 1956); Albert Lauterbach, *Man, Motives and Money* (2nd ed., Cornell University Press, 1954); Jacques Leclercq, *Christianity and Money* (Hawthorn Books, 1959); Remy G. Kwant, *Philosophy of Labor* (Duquesne University, 1960).

5 HONESTY AND TRUTHFULNESS

COLLOQUIAL AMERICAN ENGLISH is rich in words for what are ordinarily considered dishonest practices. Payola, graft, the fix, the kickback, form part of our working vocabulary even when they are not part of our personal lives. Though the prevalence of such words does not prove that our age outdoes others in villainy, it does indicate that honesty still remains a problem. A glance at the newspapers, the best-seller list, the Bulletins of the Better Business Bureau or of the Federal Trade Commission only confirms this. Indeed, at times, it almost seems that our age has discovered new ways of cheating, even though we may not have created a "new sin."[1]

Price fixing, old confidence games, phony C.O.D. practices, short measure, wholesale and retail bribery, are still around and flourishing so luxuriantly that a few professional writers manage to make a nice living by exposing them to the public. The public, for its part, gobbles all of this up, because such news either titillates the curiosity or provides them living models for their own ideas. Some are sincerely shocked by it, but they are probably not the majority. After all, cheating is so common in private life, in the home, in schools and in circles of friends, that an honest man of the good old fashioned sort sometimes seems a rarity.

While it is difficult to assess the extent of dishonesty in either business or private life, it seems clear that the problem is wide-spread. Sorokin, writing well over twenty years ago, noted that the whole contractual and fiducial framework of society seemed to be decaying.[2] The crisis in marriage reflects this, as do the repeated upheavals in the international order. This trend, together with a desire to avoid suffering at all costs, has produced a moral atmosphere in which honesty becomes a question of convenience, expediency or social conformity, rather than a matter of principle. No wonder then, if the business world suffers from the same disease.

All this, however, should not blind us to the fact that most people, including most businessmen, think of themselves as being basically honest. The majority probably make a good deal of effort to be honest in large areas of their activity, and this although the line between right and wrong is often blurred in the popular conscience. Strangely enough honesty is still admired and many who admit to being "operators" themselves prefer to deal with an honest man.

In all frankness, one must admit that it is not easy to be honest any more. In the first place, the honest man must often pay a price for his virtue. In the second, it has become increasingly difficult to decide what is honest and what is dishonest. This results not only from a general confusion about morals, but from a loss of the old rules of thumb that worked fifty years ago but just do not seem to apply today. Even the professional moralist can have difficulties in this field for the simple reason that the facts are hard to come by. Certainly, we may *feel* uneasy about a certain way of acting, but is it really dishonest?

To a certain extent the civil law still helps us to answer this question. But there are anomalies in the law which serve to increase uneasiness. Gambling is illegal, but you must pay taxes on your winnings. Kickbacks would appear to be dishonest, yet, according to some courts, you can escape paying taxes on them.

Despite the self-assurance of those who say they intuitively know what is right and wrong, honest and dishonest, questions of justice and truthfulness are often difficult. Seminary textbooks in moral theology, for example, give more space to the question of justice than to any other. Even experienced moralists want time to study and consult before answering what may appear to be simple questions in this area.

Despite the confusion and the intrinsic difficulties of some cases, a clearer understanding of even a few basic principles can narrow the area of doubt by showing the businessman what factors are important from an ethical point of view. He may still have to consult an expert on ethics about the more thorny problems, but he will be able to handle most everyday cases.

Honesty

An honest man is one who is ready to give each man his due. If he has this attitude, he has the virtue of justice. Obviously, this virtue demands a deep and real concern for the rights of others. It presupposes foresight, lest we inadvertently harm another, and demands humility, lest we exaggerate our own rights. Most of all, it requires a sound sense of values, a sense of moral proportion and self-respect. In practice, moreover, justice may call for heroic self-sacrifice since expediency must be sacrificed to principle and personal gain to personal integrity.

All this is true and beautiful. What, however, is a man's due in a given set of circumstances? How, moreover, do I go about determining what is his due? These are the difficult questions which make the practice of honesty a burden even to the mind.

In the first place, law and agreements, both explicit and implicit, can help to determine what is due and just. Often, industry custom can be helpful in determining the conditions implicit in a verbal business agreement. Many problems can be solved if relationships have been determined precisely from the very beginning of a business affair. For this reason, industry codes and well-written company policies are very useful, even if some refuse to follow them.

The following provision from *Standards for Buying and Selling*, sponsored by the National Association of Purchasing Agents, illustrates the utility, albeit limited, of explicit determinations.

To provide or accept no gifts or entertainment in the guise of sales expenses, where the intent or the effect is to unduly prejudice the recipient in favor of the donor as against legitimate competitors.

Actually, such a provision only sets a minimum norm, and many companies forbid the giving or receiving of all gifts. The reasoning behind such policies is well illustrated by the following statement from one national firm.

As it is impossible to differentiate between the gifts which may bias an employee's judgment and those which do not, company policy prohibits the acceptance of any gifts by employees from any supplier of goods or services, including consultants.

Experience shows that such strictness is wise for yet another reason. Once gift giving becomes common, even customary, some are tempted to demand them, so that even legitimate gifts may lead to extortion. This point is important for it shows that in determining the morality of many acts, we must look not only at the act itself, but at the type of situation which it may create. When a good act may breed trouble, there is an obligation to avoid it, except when there is a serious reason for risking it.

In all cases of this type, it is necessary to look beyond the immediate present, for the real evils often appear only in time. This was certainly the case in the payola scandals where gifts became bribes and where bribes led to deceiving the public and to the creation of an unfair pattern of competition.

To be completely realistic, we must recognize that much dishonesty is bred by incompetence, cowardice and myopia. In the world of business, one tends to give rise to the other. Incompetence tempts men to hide their mistakes by trickery and dishonesty. Other men, afraid that the trickster will take away their business, follow suit. Both forget that the short-run profit will disappear when their incompetence comes to light and their dishonesty leads to a loss of business. We can illustrate this problem by looking at the case of the advertising salesman who promises too much because he does not understand the functions or limits of advertising, and the capacity of his own agency. Both the salesman and the agency may be tempted to use bribery in an effort to get results, and to demand "kickbacks" in an attempt to make a profit. In the long run, the salesman will be fired, and the company, if it doesn't lose business, will certainly lose face. The outcome is that profits will fall off.

The force of cowardice is well illustrated by the ancient and dishonorable battle cry "cheat or starve." During the Payola Investigations many record companies replied to the FTC charges by stating that if they did not bribe disk jockeys their competitors would get all the business. As a matter of fact, we know that the record industry fell into a pattern of competition in which trickery was substituted for value. Once this pattern was established only the bravest and biggest of men had the courage to oppose it. It is important to note that cowardice can breed this sort of impossible situation.

The myopic approach to business is probably most characteristic of the firm which is poorly financed and feels that it must make a quick killing or go into bankruptcy. These firms feel that "ethics are a luxury." Hypnotized by this situation and this slogan, they forget that repeat sales depend on public confidence and that temporary success may be the very thing which will destroy long-range profits.

In addition to the three fundamental weaknesses I have mentioned, there is a fourth which seems to be American. I refer to the attitude that the evil other men do is not one's concern. In its most extreme form, this attitude causes men to stand by and watch hoodlums attack an elderly person. In business, it leads to a practical tolerance of even widespread dishonesty. I say "practical tolerance" because the very people who act as spectators are often the most noisy in denouncing these same evils. Because of this attitude, many businessmen do not organize in such a way as to make effective self-policing a reality. They allow the scoundrels to continue unimpeded. As a result, the public tars all businessmen with the same brush. The honest, like it or not, must wear the same black eye as the dishonest.

A scrutiny of one's motives will often show that an act is dishonest even though there are rationalizations to justify it. Often too, you can test an act by asking if you would want it disclosed to superiors, to the public or to the government.[3] Such a test is not conclusive, but can serve to unmask the feebleness of many excuses for entering into the grey areas.

An awareness of the effects of one's acts and a frank recognition of one's weaknesses and motives can help in making ethical decisions. For all that, there are difficult cases. The problems connected with commercial espionage and executive piracy would seem to fall into this class. Yet even here, one can settle most of the questions with the basic norms we have given above. Thus, if the collection of competitive information involves misrepresentation, fraud, bribery, burglary or theft, it is obviously dishonest. So too, the use of undercover agents is clearly an attempt to violate another company's clear right to privacy.[4] Finally, any type of act which would tend to lead to the above activities is to be avoided as dishonest.

What must be stressed is that difficulty in making some decisions does not mean that there are no principles whatsoever. Often only more experience of the effects of an act is needed to pass a certain judgment about the ethical quality of doubtful and difficult situations. The obligation, then, will be to investigate, rather than deciding by omission and postponement.

Honesty as a Business Virtue

Honesty costs something. It demands sacrifice of what appear to be opportunities for gain. It calls for courage. Sometimes, it exposes one to the ridicule of those who follow the rule of the mob or the line of least resistance. Often, the costs seem so great that men overlook the fact that the rewards of honesty are greater than its cost. I do not mean merely that honesty pays off in moral growth, well founded self-respect and a tranquil conscience. This of course is the real reward of honesty. I mean that even as a purely business virtue, honesty is the best policy in the long run.

The words *in the long run* are important, for the temptation is always to consider the immediate loss or gain and to forget that business is a continuing proposition. The company out to make a quick killing is generally quickly killed. Dishonesty has a way of catching up with corporations as well as individuals, so that the gain, even in a monetary sense, is soon gone.

On the other hand a reputation for honesty and fair dealing is a business asset. A man's credit rating depends on this, as do repeat sales, promotion to positions of trust, and recognition both in and out of business. Honesty also attracts other honest people, rather than operators and fly-by-nighters who are willing to throw anyone to the wolves.

One is continually struck by the observation that though many honest businessmen have problems, and even admit to having made wrong moral decisions, they tend to agree that they have never regretted a decision made on moral principle.

Truthfulness

A great many problems in business ethics involve the question of truthfulness. Often, the problems are exaggerated because of ignorance of basic principles and of general obligations. Consequently, it is necessary at least to sketch the more fundamental aspects of lying.

Lying is condemned by any sound ethics. There is, however, some disagreement as to what constitutes a *lie*. Some define it as speech against one's mind; others as speech against one's communicable mind. This latter definition implies that a lie is not to be equated simply with a *falsehood*. The moral evil comes into existence when the falsehood is told in circumstances where the other person has an objectively grounded expectation of the truth. This definition recognizes that others do not generally have a legitimate and grounded expectation that one will reveal secret information. Even those who use the simpler definition (speech against the mind), admit that you can conceal *legitimate* secrets by evasions, silence, or broad mental reservations: that is, by speech which represents one's mind, but can be given another meaning by the listener. When a secretary tells a caller that her employer is not in, she is using a broad mental reservation. Her real meaning is that he is not in to the caller. Nearly everyone recognizes this, and would not call her reply a lie. The second definition will permit outright *falsehood* in some situations, for example when a spy is being questioned. In such a case there is no reasonable expectation of the truth and so no *lie*, that is, no moral evil.

No matter what definition is used, sound ethics permits a man to conceal company secrets. Evasion and silence are to be preferred to the broad mental reservation, and the broad mental reservation is to be used rather than outright falsehood, but the right to protect the secret remains. At the same time, it should be noted that though you may protect secrets, you have no right to use deception and falsehoods to gain the upper hand of a competitor. The use of false rumors, for example, is certainly to be condemned as lying. So too, the consumer cannot be deceived on the ground that the defects of a product are a company secret. The consumer has an objectively founded expectation of the truth.

Advertising

The professional codes of the Chamber of Commerce and the advertising associations recognize the obligation to be truthful. The Advertising Code of the International Chamber of Commerce, for example, contains these provisions.

3. Advertising should tell the truth and avoid distorting facts and misleading by means of implications and omissions.
4. No advertisement should be permitted to contain any claim so exaggerated as to lead inevitably to disappointment in the mind of the consumer.
5. False or misleading statements as to personal recommendation of the firm, product or service advertised must not be employed.

Though these, or similar provisions, can be found in most codes, the interpretations given to these words depend in large part on the general level of business morality, and on the legal codes which are also in force. In Germany, for example, even superlatives are suspect, while in the United States such words as *the best, the world's finest,* are considered as no more than legitimate, because meaningless, puffery. Similarly the interpretation will vary if the rules are held to apply only to substantial deceptions or to any false impression whatever. Some, of course, consider an advertisement misleading only when it deceives a *normally prudent man,* while others say that a truthful advertisement should not lead even the simple astray. All these different points of view are reflected in various legal decisions as well as in business practice. There are signs that today the general trend is towards a rather strict interpretation. This is clearly reflected in the following norms laid down by the Advertising Federation of America in *The Advertising Truth Book* prepared by Morton J. Simon, their Associate General Counsel.[5]

It has been suggested that an advertiser, judging the honesty of his sales message, need only ask himself a few direct questions:

Is it *really* honest?

Is it *clear* to the people who hear it or look at it?

Can I *prove* all this?

Would I approve if my *competitor* used this copy?

Is this *straight* talk?

Would I want *my* wife to spend *my* money because of this ad?

Have I cut out *all* weaseling?

If the answer to *all* of these pointed questions can be a strong *Yes*, then you can be pretty sure that the advertising is legitimate, legal, truthful, meaningful, clear . . . yes . . . and also believable and productive.

The author of the *Advertising Truth Book* goes even farther when he notes that advertisements should be considered in their entirety and as they would be read by those to whom they appeal. He even notes that advertisements are not meant to be dissected with the dictionary in hand, but are to produce an impression on the ordinary purchaser whether he be trusting or suspicious. In addition, omissions of points that should be revealed may make an advertisement deceptive even when every statement in it is literally true. These interpretations, strict as they are, are made even more rigid when the author lays down the general principle: "IF IN DOUBT, DON'T."

These principles are unusually strict. As a matter of fact, I know of no other professional advertising group which has adopted such clear and confining rules in the matter of truthfulness. Unfortunately, even advertisers of good will do not, and possibly cannot, live up to such norms. This is not to say that advertisers are indifferent to the truth, but that their point of view and goals are often at odds with a really strict view of what constitutes deception.

The advertiser and his agent, for example, tend to accept the following assumptions. First, an advertisement does not, and cannot, in most cases give complete information about a product. Frequently the advertisement only tells the public that such and such a product is available or that the advertiser believes his product to be the best of its kind. Secondly, since an advertisement is not technically an offer to sell and presupposes that the public can inform itself at the point of purchase, the omission of many details is of no great seriousness. In short, the advertiser assumes that the public sees him as an interested party, who, while maintaining a certain good faith, does not pretend to give full information about his product. In one way, many advertisers subscribe to the old *caveat emptor*, even when they condemn any attempt at outright deception.

The advertiser also believes that he has a perfect right to use what he considers the accepted idiom of advertising. This is not as foolish as it might seem, since even children realize that the same word has one meaning when used by an advertiser, another when used by members of their own family. The exaggerations of advertising, then, are not necessarily deceptive in context, but only when taken literally and in the abstract.

Even the honest advertiser does not intend to speak to everyone. He addresses his message to a given group, though he knows others will receive it. He speaks to a hypothetical normal man in that group and tends to disregard the gullible, since he can do nothing about fools and spendthrifts. Indeed, the advertiser knows all too well that it is almost impossible to word a message so that it will be unambiguous to all members of his potential audience.

Over and beyond these points of view is the fact that the advertiser operates more often than not in the realm of opinion, not in the realm of truth. He is not merely describing objective facts, but attempting to convince someone that his opinion about his own product is correct. Such opinions are not capable of any absolute proof, or even of verification; but if they are sincere, they are not necessarily deceptive.

Finally, and this is of the utmost importance, most advertisers consider an advertisement deceptive only when it creates a false impression about some important aspect of the product or service.[6] In other words, there is deception only when the false understanding generated by the advertisement influences buying behavior in some significant respect. Let me illustrate.

A false endorsement by a movie star would constitute deception since her statement provides a motive for buying and is understood in that light. However, the appearance of a professional model does not constitute deception because she does not give professional approval of the product, that is, does not intend to provide a prime motive for buying. Of course, the model's presence implies that beautiful women use the product, but since this is probably true, there is no real problem for the advertiser. It would be quite another question if the product promised to make every woman beautiful and offered a refund in case of failure.

It is rather hard to quarrel with the advertiser's perspective since it has been well established in the commercial practice of many nations. For all this, there is a dispute precisely because the public, and especially its vocal members, have a different point of view.

The Public's Viewpoint

Where the advertisers tend to concentrate on the best representatives of their profession, while admitting that there is a small but persistent amount of deceptive advertising, the public is all too familiar with the deceptive practices of many local merchants and fly-by-night operators who place their announcements in the shadier journals. The public and the critics of advertising, moreover, concentrate their attention on certain classes of advertisements which are almost of their very nature deceptive. Patent medicine advertising, reducing ads, announcements of cures for baldness or for poorly developed breasts, as well as much movie advertising, promise more than they can deliver. Since the public is subject to a great deal of such advertising, it tends to attribute the defects of these to advertising as a whole.

The public is becoming increasingly sophisticated and better educated. It tends to judge advertising not merely on what it says, or on what it can reasonably be taken to say, but on the basis of the long-range impression which the advertiser wants to create. Everyone knows that smoking cigarettes will not make one distinguished, masculine or admired, but they also know that the advertiser would like to create just such an impression. This is considered to be basically dishonest and all advertising is judged accordingly. Indeed, if such a norm is legitimate, much if not all, consumer advertising might be considered deceptive, at least in intent.

The sophisticated public is also aware that the advertiser would like to establish an opinion monopoly by so dominating memory and attention that the idea of competing products is lost in a welter of sound and visual impressions. This, too, is taken as part of a deceptive strategy and judged accordingly.

Finally, I believe that the general public equates the meaninglessness of much advertising with deception. Certainly the bottles of beer X are washed in live steam, but so are the bottles of most other beers. Of course, cigarette Y has a new magic filter, but so does brand Z. All this, the consumer feels, is an attempt to convince him that a difference exists, where no real difference can be found. "Your claims are meaningless, if true, but are at the same time, part of a campaign to fool me." This is the consumers' reaction.

In short, the public has quite different ideas from the advertiser as to what constitutes deception. The public is not satisfied with *caveat emptor,* nor with the idiom of advertising, nor with the literal truthfulness of what is said. It demands, albeit often mutely, a higher standard of business morality.

Specialized groups in consumers' unions, in education or economics are, to be sure, far stricter than the general public. These people realize that such things as an opinion monopoly, false impressions or meaningless differences can lead to economic losses, to adverse effects on price, quality and the variety of goods available. Therefore they are quite vocal in condemning what the advertiser would consider an honest advertisement. Since many of these critics are in positions where they can influence public opinion, their views tend to strengthen it against advertising and to intensify the quarrel over what constitutes truth in advertising.

A Meeting of Minds

Any attempt to decide between the opposed points of view is doomed to failure. From a strictly legal viewpoint the advertisers are probably far on the safe side in the vast majority of cases. In terms of traditional, individualistic ethical principles, much advertising is either legitimate or only slightly objectionable on grounds of truthfulness. The problem, however, is not merely legal, or ethical in an individualistic sense. It is a problem in professional ethics and in social understanding.

When I say it is a problem in professional ethics, I mean that it is a question of whether or not the standards used by advertising are harming the profession, even when they work no real harm on the public. When I speak of a problem in social understanding, I refer to difficulties which arise in the communication structures of a society when there is a lack of agreement about the terms of discourse.

Though my opinion is subject to correction, I believe that the profession suffers from a lack of public trust. Even though people continue to read and follow advertisements, the aura of mistrust tends to diminish the effectiveness of the announcements and to tempt the borderline operator to continue his corner cutting. So long as public trust is necessary for the functioning of the economy and of the distributive sector in particular, anything that disturbs this must be considered an evil, for both the society and the professions engaged in sales.

The arguments used to justify the position of the advertisers are, within certain limits, valid. Indeed, in another age where *caveat emptor* was still an accepted principle not only of law but of public life, the arguments may have been completely valid. It is useless, however, to talk about the validity of the case, if the public refuses to accept it, and continues to mistrust those who are attempting to defend themselves.

In view of this, *The Advertising Truth Book* is probably a step in the right direction. Though it is far stricter than previous codes, and far above the level of actual commercial practice, it does approach the norms which the public tends to use in judging advertising. If its rules can be reduced to practice, the areas of disagreement can be narrowed considerably and confidence increased.

It must be admitted, however, that even the strictest code and most vigorous enforcement cannot solve all the problems connected with truthfulness in advertising. So long as language, and symbols, and the meaning of things, themselves, remain ambiguous, there will always be a certain, and possibly a large, area of dispute. So long, too, as special pleading remains basically legitimate, and opinion a valid, and even useful, part of discourse, there will be differences of opinion about what is and what is not deceptive.

Reform

Even though we admit an area of legitimate debate, and recognize the impossibility of complete agreement, there are still positive and practical steps which can be taken to reduce misunderstanding and increase the utility of advertising.

In the first place, there is a need to educate advertisers, their agents, and the owners of the mass media, to the real state of public opinion and of unexpressed public attitudes toward advertising. There seems to be a cultural lag here, since public concepts have passed beyond those of the business world. This may sound quixotic, but many professionals in both Europe and the United States agree that there is need to educate the advertisers in particular. After all, they hold the whip hand, and without their cooperation there can be no reform.

In the second place, all professionals engaged in advertising must realize that in the case of patent medicines, cigarettes, personal products and similar articles, there is probably need for a strengthening of the law which governs their advertisement. Indeed, as a general rule, there is need for legislation in the case of all products where deception can harm the health as well as the pocketbook of the consumer. Unfortunately, the powerful groups of advertisers who sell these products have in the past often obstructed such legislation. This does not diminish the responsibility of the profession to protect both itself and the public in these areas.

Thirdly, there is need for a non-government group to pass on the truthfulness of advertisements before they are published. Though such a group would be expensive (it would need a large staff, testing facilities, etc.), it would repay advertisers by raising public confidence in their messages. Though preliminary steps to establish such groups have been limited, there is every reason to suspect that they can be effective, even if they cannot eliminate all abuses.

There are other suggestions that might be made. Advertising has not done everything that is possible and even reasonable in protecting the public. At the same time we must recognize that the professionals have in most countries moved increasingly to stricter standards and are not, except in a very few cases, the villains they are sometimes painted.

Notes

1. *Cf.* Frank Gibney, *The Operators* (Harper and Brothers, 1960).
2. Pitirim A. Sorokin, *The Crisis of Our Age* (E. P. Dutton, 1941), chapter V.
3. *Cf.* Controllers Institute of America, *Conflict of Interest,* March 2, 1961, p. 6.
4. *Cf.* Burton H. Alden *et al., Competitive Intelligence* (Watertown, Mass.: C. I. Associates, 1959), p. 60.
5. Morton J. Simon, *The Advertising Truth Book,* AFA, 1960.
6. Certain FTC decisions are based on stricter norms. As a result advertisers should make sure that they consult their lawyers as well as their consciences.

Readings

For some case work in the area of honesty *cf.* Catholic Employers and Managers Study Groups, *Operating and Meeting Guide,* Chicago, 1962 (mimeographed); Herbert Johnston, *Business Ethics*

(Pitman, 1961); James Marvin Lee, *Business Ethics* (Ronald Press, 1926); Frank Chapman Sharp and Philip G. Fox, *Business Ethics* (D. Appleton-Century, 1937), and Henry J. Wirtenberger, S.J., *Morality and Business* (Chicago: Loyola University, 1962).

On the advertising *cf.* Thomas M. Garrett, S.J., *An Introduction to Some Ethical Problems of Modern American Advertising* (Rome: Gregorian University Press, 1961).

6 THE WORLD OF THE EXPENSE ACCOUNT

THOUGH MANY PROBLEMS connected with expense accounts are questions of simple honesty, the whole matter is so complicated that it deserves a chapter by itself. This is particularly true since popular exposé type articles have served to confuse the issue rather than to shed real light on the ethical problems involved. The bothersome problems of the businessman center less on the company yacht and the company hunting lodge than on the ordinary day-by-day questions of acceptable business practice, allowable expenses for travel, and the relation of the expense account to the tax report.

While the expense account is a day-by-day problem, it has not been treated extensively by professional moralists. Worse yet, amateur moralists have often confused the businessman by giving him strange advice. Some dismiss most of the problems by saying that the tax laws do not bind in conscience. Others assure businessmen that if they pay seventy percent of their taxes they are in the clear. A third group ignores the obligations which executives have to their stockholders, or canonizes accepted business practice.

These opinions do not solve the problems. Despite the prevalence of such lax positions, the businessman still feels uneasy. About half the respondents in the Harvard Business Review Survey of 1960 were disturbed by the tax-related expense account practices of their opposite numbers.[1] A second Harvard Business Review Survey in 1961 indicated that 86% of the respondents regarded the padding of expense accounts as always unethical.[2] This is encouraging since it indicates that this aspect of justice still receives at least lip service. What, however, is meant by "Padding"? Why are businessmen uneasy about tax-related uses of expense accounts? What principles should govern expense accounts in general?

It is not easy to give answers to any of these questions since the meaning of the words varies with the type of expense account used, the policy of the company and the interpretation of tax law at a given moment. Some information is needed about these matters before any attempt is made to lay down principles or solve cases.

Moral problems involving expense accounts can arise from one or more of the following relationships: first, the relation of the recipient to the company; second, the relation of the grantor to both the recipient and the company; third, the relation of both the recipient and the company to the tax laws. In judging any actual case, all these relationships must be studied.

For purposes of clarity, we can divide expense accounts into four general classes or combinations thereof. The first type involves the reimbursement by the company for expenses *already* incurred by an employee. A second type consists of billing the company directly. A third type is found in the flat annual payment in addition to salary which the employee need not account for, but which he presumably uses for business expenses. The fourth, and last, type is the *per diem* allowance which, like the annual payment, need not be accounted for.

From an ethical point of view each of these types poses its own problems. Where the first two types are used, the employee is responsible for the validity of the claims he makes on the company, while the company is responsible for the tax aspects— except where the expense account allows expenses which neither the company nor the individual can deduct from income. The third and fourth types free the recipient from an obligation to account to the company, but make him liable for the tax on any income not spent for deductible items.

Though we are primarily interested in the ethical problems connected with expense accounts, it should be noted that the expense account is also subject to economic and business norms, as well as to accounting norms of accuracy. Consequently, good business practice as well as ethics should be considered.

The Recipient and the Company

Essentially, an expense account is payment for asset value consumed in furthering the interests of the firm. In general, the recipient's right to such payment will depend on company policy, that is, on the contractual relation, explicit or implicit, between the employee and his employer. In particular, it will also depend on accepted accounting principles and on the type of expense account involved.

When dealing with expense allowances, whether *per diem* or annual, there are no great problems. The recipient in such cases may pocket what is left over after he has spent what he should on behalf of the company. However, if the company expects him to stay at the best hotels for reasons of prestige, he is not fulfilling his obligations if he uses less expensive hotels. Obviously, there is room for judgment in these cases and no hard and fast rule can be drawn.

When the expense account demands repayment item by item, or when the company is billed directly, the principle is simply this: an employee has a right to repayment for money legitimately spent on behalf of the company. To demand more is to steal. Most companies have some sort of policy and this should be consulted. As a rule, these policies stress the idea that an employee should live as comfortably on the road as at home, and should not suffer any monetary loss because of his travel.[3] Though all of this is simple enough in the abstract, the real world is filled with grey areas and difficult cases. A few examples may help to indicate the type of circumstances which should be considered in making particular judgments.

A junior executive, who plays cards rather well, is ordered to lose so as to gain a client's good will. May he do this? May he claim reimbursement on his expense account? Can he disguise his claim by putting it under some heading such as travel or entertainment?

A representative sample of businessmen, when asked to comment on this case, noted that it involved hidden commercial bribery. They felt, and rightly, that it would be unethical to lose at cards with such a purpose in mind. Moreover, it would, if widespread, lead to other abuses.

If we prescind from the question of bribery, the gambling loss was authorized and so is reimbursable in simple justice. However, because such a claim would not be recognized by the accounting department, the loser can get back his money only by demanding it under some accepted heading. This however, could easily lead the accountants to demand a deduction which is not allowable. The only solution would be to put it under a heading which the company will allow but which will not result in an illegal claim for a deduction from taxes.

This case is interesting not only because it shows that several factors must be considered, but because it demonstrates how dishonesty can breed other problems. Here as elsewhere, integrity at the beginning of a transaction will prevent the growth of moral difficulties.

Some expense account problems revolve around the wife who accompanies her husband on a business trip. These problems are all the more difficult because they generally involve upper management which sets the policy in the first instance. According to one study,[4] seventy-three percent of married executives in top management said that their wives accompanied them on trips, while only forty-five and one half percent of lower middle management enjoyed this privilege. It is interesting to note, however, that the top executives reported a wide variety of company policies. Forty-seven percent said that the company allowed them to use the family plan and to pay the difference themselves. Forty-four percent said that the company paid for the wives only when it had requested their presence. In thirty-four percent of the cases, the companies paid only when the wife was performing a customer function or a company service. Others footed the bill when the trip was relatively long and for employee relations.

Though there is a good deal of variety, the underlying principle seems to be that the expense is tax deductible when the wife is giving some sort of service. So long as there is service, and company authorization, the expenditure would seem to be reasonable. When, however, the wives' main activity is meeting other wives or enjoying the ladies' program which is a part of many conventions, both the government and the stockholders may have doubts about the justification of having the wife's bills paid out of the firm's funds. Despite these doubts, there are good reasons for the company to allow such expenses, even when the wife does not perform some service *directly and immediately* related to the good of the firm. Long and frequent absences from his home many damage the morale of an employee; so the presence of his wife can be of real, if indirect, value to the company.

Similar cases arise with regard to the use of company farms, resorts and dummy branch offices in vacation-land, all of which may be unrelated to any immediate contribution to the company. If we leave out the accounting and tax-related aspects of this problem, such expenses can often be legitimate. A company has a real interest in the health of its top executives, who are often unique and almost irreplaceable. Consequently, an investment in the preservation of the executive can often be a legitimate expense, from a business point of view.

The list of practices which could be discussed is almost endless. There is the use of company cars and planes for private
purposes; the mutual luncheon club, and the payment of club
dues, even when the club is seldom if ever used for company
business. When the expense is for the benefit of the company, or
approved as part of the employees' compensation, the recipient's
conscience need not be disturbed. When, however, there is no
real service to the company, or when the reimbursement is obtained without approval or under false pretenses, we are once
again dealing with a form of theft.

Company Policy

The executives who must pass on the validity of expense accounts have an obligation to work for the good of the company
and for its owners. This means that expenses can be allowed only
in so far as they contribute to the good of the firm. In other
words, they cannot use company money as their own. The same
is true when a firm is acting as agent for another and is paid on a
cost-plus basis. In addition, executives must pay attention to the
tax laws and to good accounting practice.[5] In setting policy,
then, they must ask two questions. 1) Is this expense for the
good of the company? 2) To what extent is this expense allowable as a tax deduction?

The law and industry custom will help to answer these questions, but from time to time a more careful checkup may be
necessary. The reason is simply that laws change and customs
can become abuses.

Granted that there is room for expenditures to protect the
health of the executive and to maintain his morale while traveling, most ethical and business and legal problems can be solved

if the companies adhere to the three rules set down by H. C. Smith in the *Harvard Business Review*.[6]

1. The expenditure must have a definite and proximate relationship to a particular business enterprise.
2. The expenditure must be both reasonable and necessary.
3. The expenditure must be substantiated in a satisfactory manner.

The first two rules are really norms of good business practice. The third rule is an accounting norm which is very necessary today in view of the requirement that tax allowable items be substantiated in the corporation's records to support claims for tax deductions. The first rules are also ethical insofar as they guarantee that the executive is safeguarding the company and fulfilling his obligations to the stockholders, or to his principal when he is acting as an agent. These same norms can be used by employees when deciding whether or not they have a right to claim reimbursement for expenses.

Nearly everything we have said so far revolves around the inflation of expense accounts. Often (it is hard to estimate how often), companies err by a stinginess which forces employees to lose money and to suffer when on trips. This can lead not only to chronic injustice on the part of the company but to the encouragement of cheating on the part of the employee. Unless it is clearly understood that an employee is to pay his own expenses, there is an obligation to reimburse him for those which are direct and necessary costs of his furthering the interests of the company.

The Obligation to Pay Taxes

Many of the most thorny problems connected with the expense account concern the obligation of the corporation and the individual to pay taxes. Some claim that the tax laws do not bind you to pay the tax in conscience, but only to pay the penalty if you are caught. Some claim that there is no obligation because the laws are unjust. Yet others excuse themselves on the ground that tax revenues are wasted. The confusion in this area is so great that even men of good will often do not know where they stand.

There can be no doubt that there is an obligation in conscience to pay some taxes. There is, however, a great deal of dispute as to whether one is obliged to pay all taxes imposed by civil law.[7] The question, then, cannot be settled by an appeal to authority.

While granting that an individual may follow the opinion of authorities whose arguments convince him, the following considerations seem to point to an obligation to pay all just taxes; and to assume that all taxes are just, unless conclusively proved otherwise.

Individuals and corporations have an obligation to support the common good by making financial contributions. Since the nature and amount of their contribution are not determined by the very structure of existence, the government has the right and obligation to specify these. Once the nature and amount have been specified, there is an obligation to obey the law, since the common good can be attained only if men cooperate in this way. Granted that penalties are necessary to assure the payment of taxes, the ultimate source of cooperation is a respect for law and an acceptance of the goal of the law. Consequently, a theory which relies only on the effectiveness of penalties and denies that there is a moral obligation to obey the civil law itself, would appear to be breaking down one of the basic foundations of social life.

Some contend that our taxes are unjust, discriminatory and even tyrannical. Granted that there is no obligation to pay unjust taxes, the existence of injustice is to be proved rather than assumed. Further, for the argument to be valid, the injustice must be substantial. After all, it is of the very nature of human positive law to be imperfect. If *any and every* inequity excuses a citizen, then all laws will have to go out the window. The existence of inequalities and hardship cases, which are fairly numerous in the United States, proves only that the income tax laws in general are fallible and human, not that they are unjust as a whole.

Unless we wish to destroy all law, the presupposition must always be that our laws are just until proved otherwise. The proof, moreover, must be conclusive. The complaints of friends or the propaganda of interested parties does not establish the conclusion that the law need not be obeyed. If such evidence were admissible, no law would be universally valid and we would have anarchy on our hands.

Today people are prone to excuse themselves on the ground that they are not obliged to pay because many others are avoiding their obligations. The evidence, however, seems to be against them. The Internal Revenue Service, for example, estimates that only about one percent of potential tax payers fail to file returns.[8] Further, it is estimated that only about four percent of the taxes called for under law are unreported and unpaid.[9] This would hardly seem to constitute an excuse for not obeying the law. Some accountants note that there is more boasting about evasion of taxes than actual evasion. It would appear that while it is fashionable to claim that you are cheating, most people are actually conscientious.

None of this should be taken to mean that the income tax laws are perfect, or even just, in all their provisions. There is undoubtedly need for reform.[10] What must be stressed, however, is that the law is basically just and so to be obeyed.

Others hold that there is no obligation to pay in full when tax money is being wasted. Aside from the fact that waste seems to be seriously exaggerated, the person who wants to use such an excuse must answer such questions as the following, before he can proceed to act in good conscience.[11] How much of his tax burden results from graft? How much graft is there? Does it amount to even two percent of our tax levy? Has any investigation even suggested that it is one percent? If the amount of graft is relatively small, is he still justified in evading taxes on this score? If so, how much may *he* dodge?

These are serious questions and one cannot by-pass them without serious imprudence and contempt for law in general. Even if we grant that moralists do justify disobedience to unjust laws, their principles cannot be followed unless the facts prove that the case they envision is actually present in the United States. As Philip S. Land, S.J., professor of social ethics at the Gregorian University, has put it:

I recognize that even against the weight of my argument those who disagree may rest their freedom on the support of recognized authorities. But it cannot too emphatically be insisted that no theologian is a valid authority *unless he is talking about a situation identifiable as the equivalent of what we have seen exists here in the United States.*[12]

Even if a man feels that he has no obligation to pay taxes, for any one of a variety of reasons, he may still be bound out of charity to himself and his family. Violations can bring prosecution for tax evasion leading to fines and imprisonment, and no man can risk these without a serious reason. To run such risks without a proportionate reason is immoral, even aside from the more basic consideration of the social obligation to support the body politic.

In practice, the question of the obligation to pay income taxes is clarified by yet another consideration.[13] Even those authorities who claim that the American Income Tax Laws do not bind in conscience admit that evasion necessarily involves fraud, deceit and lying. Unless a tax is monumentally and unequivocally unjust, such means cannot be considered.

These considerations do not pretend to settle the question once and for all. Individual cases demand individual study. What must be stressed is that in general there is an obligation to pay income taxes. In practice, at least, there seems to be no such thing as a blanket excuse or a moral way of evading them. Both individuals and corporations can morally take advantage of the deductions allowed by law. *Avoidance* of taxes is permitted. What is to be condemned is the *evasion* of taxes, that is the effort to escape the actual provisions of the law. It should also be remembered that from a moral point of view, evasion is evasion even if the government cannot establish it in a court of law. When a man acts against his conscience, he is guilty whether caught or not.

The Expense Account and Taxes

Granted this, the case of the expense account seems to be fairly simple in the abstract. If expenses are directly and proximately related to the course of business and are moreover necessary and ordinary, they may, with some exceptions, be deducted from income, the tax being paid on the remainder. In practice, unfortunately, things are not quite so simple. In the first place, it is not always easy to judge whether an expense is direct, ordinary and necessary; in the second place, the tactics of some Internal Revenue Agents make honesty very expensive.

Ordinarily, the businessman should be able to judge the nature of his expenses in terms of his own experience and of sound industry practice. This is still a good rule of thumb. Unfortunately some groups have fallen into dubious practices. I do not refer to such obviously immoral expenses as those incurred by bribery, espionage, call-girls and the mutual luncheon club, but to the widespread tendency to use the expense account as *hidden* compensation. Such practices are obviously attempts to evade the law and as such unethical.

In judging intent, the businessman should ask himself if this expense account really covers expenses or is intended as a fringe benefit or as part of the employee's salary. If his intention is correct, and honest accountants concur, he has done his best in forming a correct conscience.

When all is said and done, there still remain large grey areas. Even a man of good will cannot always tell what is avoidance and permitted, and what is evasion and forbidden. Business, however, will do well not to occupy the grey area, for this might tempt the government to revoke privileges and to tighten up the law. In December of 1959 the Internal Revenue Service had already announced a new program to curb abuses which, as Commissioner Dana Latham noted, tended not only to cause a loss of revenue, but to arouse a deep resentment on the part of the tax payer, who felt that his neighbor was getting a better break than he. It was just this fear of government redefining the grey area that left the businessmen in the Furash survey a bit uneasy.[14] They realized that the common good of society demanded a certain restraint on the part of their fellows.

Difficult problems arise when the tax agent enters the picture. To some extent, promotion in the Internal Revenue Service was, until recently, supposed to depend on results, and results meant recovering taxes. The field agent, if not out to get the businessman, at least tried to cut down exemptions and deductions, that is, to detect evasion. Many businessmen, of course, have taken this to be an attack, and feel that they have been deprived of legitimate deductions. Often, however, the fault has been with the businessman who has kept inadequate records and cannot justify his deductions. On the other hand, it can be that the agent has not known his business and may have used his bargaining power in order to reduce the claims.

Now that promotions no longer depend on success in reclaiming money, much of this may disappear. Certainly, every effort should be made to eliminate a situation in which confidence and open dealing are made impossible, and both sides are tempted to play hide-and-seek.

If there are real problems in this area, and some business-men seem to think there are, the solution is to be found in an organized effort to work out acceptable procedures. The use of mental reservations, the inflation of deductions so that one can give in to the agent and still come out even, are not calculated to remedy anything in the long run. At best such practices can only erode good relations between business and government.

At all times the business man should remember that good ac-counting principles as well as ethics demand that his records be accurate and in order. Indeed, if the businessman gives full information to a reliable accountant, he can be sure that he has done all that is morally required by his obligation to pay taxes.

Expense Accounts and
Good Business Practice

Even if expense accounts did not create problems in both ordinary and social justice, business would have to face the fact that many practices, though customary, are creating business problems. The easy-come-easy-go mentality implicit in the idea that the government pays half has led not only to the inflation of expenses, but also to a lowering of business discipline. In the world of the "easy buck" there is a great temptation to use the expense account to cover up minor bribery or as a substitute for competence. In addition, carelessness in the control of these expenses can lead to a general neglect of costs. More than one business man has noted how the expenses spread out and ooze over into new areas.

Here and there, signs are appearing that the problem is being recognized. Many companies no longer permit business gifts as allowable expenses. This is especially true in industries that operate on a narrow margin of profit. Others are finding that the credit card can pose problems, when the company rather than the individual is billed. Because it is difficult and costly to separate business expenses from personal ones, some now insist that the employee pay the bill and put in his claim later. This does not seem to be common, and we can expect the problem of cost control to increase as the cards become more and more common.

A few companies are also recognizing that, though the expense account may be a status symbol and a fringe benefit, it does not boost morale as much as a straight salary increase. To put it another way, if a man is worth twenty thousand dollars a year, give it to him in his pay check, rather than in the form of hidden compensations which may be illegal in the first place.

Many of the practices discussed so far are justified on the grounds that they are a necessary cost of doing business. This may be true, but often they are necessary only because everyone is doing it. Much of the wining and dining is defensive in nature, a sort of keeping-up-with-Joneses in the supposedly hardheaded world of business. Unfortunately there is a built-in spiral in this sort of competition-by-entertainment. Once it starts, the other man can always do you one better. To keep pace, you have to match or surpass the lavishness of his spending. In this way what was once a novelty or a luxury can become a necessity. The end result is an increase in costs for everyone, without, however, any increase in productivity. This is bad business by any standard.

The Expense Account and Home Life

Most companies expect their men to live well on the road. They demand, in many cases, that employees maintain the prestige of the firm in their dealings with customers. This is reasonable enough, but it can pose a real problem for the executive, especially if he is still on the lower levels. Frequent forays into the world of *haute cuisine* and luxury hotels can dull the taste for home cooking and the simple cottage in the suburbs. Carelessness with the company's money can lead to carelessness in personal finance. The effort to live in two worlds and by two standards can be a real strain for some men: a taste of the high life can in the extreme case distort one's values and wreck one's life.

This weakening of values is neither necessary nor common, but the very existence of the temptation should alert the young executive to the need for balance and maturity. Indeed, it is just another case where the importance of old-fashioned virtues such as thrift, self-discipline and prudence cannot be overemphasized. Drifting in this area can lead to a gradual loss of perspective as well as to an unbalancing of personal finance. There is need then for vigilance, here as elsewhere, in the world of the expense account.

Notes

1. Edward E. Furash, "Problems in Review: Expense Accounts," *Harvard Business Review*, March-April, 1960 (vol. 38, no. 2), p. 6.
2. Raymond C. Baumhart, "Problems in Review: How Ethical Are Businessmen?" *Harvard Business Review*, July-August, 1961 (vol. 39, no. 4), p. 12.
3. Furash, *op. cit.*, p. 9.
4. *Ibid.*, pp. 14-15.
5. *Cf.* for example the series of articles in the *Journal of Accountancy* for April, 1959, and Thomas G. Higgins, "Professional Ethics: A Time for Reappraisal," *Journal of Accountancy*, March, 1962.
6. Henry Cassorte Smith, "Watch Your Expense Accounts," *Harvard Business Review*, January-February, 1958 (vol. 36, no. 1), p. 122.
7. *Cf.* Edward T. Dunn, S.J., "In Defense of the Penal Law," in

Theological Studies, March, 1957 (vol. 18, no. 1), pp. 41-59, and M. Crowe, *The Moral Obligation of Paying Taxes* (Catholic University of America, 1944).

8. *The New York Times,* Sunday, July 29, 1962, p. 172.

9. Philip M. Stern, "That Missing 4 Billion in Taxes," in *The New York Times Magazine,* April 15, 1962, p. 70.

10. *Cf.* for example, Dan Throop Smith, *Federal Tax Reform* (Mc-Graw-Hill, 1961).

11. Philip S. Land, S.J., "Evading Taxes Can't Be Justified," *Social Order,* March, 1955 (vol. 5, no. 3), pp. 121-125.

12. *Ibid.,* p. 125.

13. *Cf.* Daniel D. Lowery, "Moral Problems in Business Practice," in *Proceedings of the Sixteenth Annual Convention of the Catholic Theological Society of America,* 1961, pp. 134-140.

14. *Cf.* note 1 above.

7 THE ETHICS OF PERSONALITY TESTING IN BUSINESS

The Organization Man brought the problem of psychological testing in business out into the open.[1] William H. Whyte, Jr., the author, also proposed a partial solution in his appendix, which bore the amusing title: "How to Cheat on Personality Tests." Even though not everyone will agree with Whyte,[2] the ethician or the businessman cannot bypass the questions he has raised. This is particularly true since *The Organization Man* shows that the problem is only one reflection of the more fundamental crisis which has arisen with the growth of scientific management and scientism in general. The area of psychological testing touches on the basic problems of the individual and of responsibility. Equally important, the problem indicates how easily certain approaches to business can erode the most fundamental ethical values.

Since the use of these tests continues to increase, though not without some setbacks, it is necessary to give them some serious consideration. In 1960, for example, more than half the respondents to a Harvard Business Review questionnaire reported that their companies were using some form of tests for selecting, promoting, transferring and developing salaried personnel.[3] Since the larger companies were more prone to use them, this means that the majority of corporation employees probably have to submit to some form of testing. To be sure, some companies have

97

dropped these procedures and others have de-emphasized them, but their use remains widespread enough to make them of real interest.

The business community itself is aware of some of the ethical problems produced by the new techniques for executive selection. A fair number agree with Whyte that the trend toward conformity to an organization personality has been helped by the tests.[4] However, there seems to be less awareness of the more basic questions of secrecy, the right to privacy and the impact of these on the good of the profession of psychology. Even the American Psychological Association's excellent *Ethical Standards of Psychologists*[5] does not give explicit attention to the specific problems raised by testing. Psychologists, however, have written of the need for clarifications in this area.[6]

The Tests

For the most part, aptitude and achievement tests offer no real difficulties. Though they are of limited value, they do not attempt to probe in secret areas, but merely to supply a neat index of certain surface qualities, which puts them beyond most criticism. Further, long experience with them has taught most trained personnel their limits and shown the need for using them only as a supplement to more traditional methods such as interviews, transcripts of school marks and recommendations of employers.

Personality tests, and in particular those based on projective methods, pose quite a different problem. The projective test is based on the assumption that people reveal their personality in talking about others and in structuring unstructured situations. Thus, what I see in an ink blot, or in an ambiguously sketched cartoon, indicates what I have projected from myself into the object before me. It is not merely a question of uncovering those superficial layers of personality which are directly observable, but of penetrating to roots of which the subject himself may not be aware, and plumbing the depths of personality.

These tests, and lie detector tests as well,[7] pose an ethical problem. Does a company have the right to invade the privacy of the individual by forcing employees, or would-be employees, to submit to these tests? This is the problem of psychic privacy in a non-therapeutic situation.

There are other problems which arise from the nature of these tests and their method of interpretation. Though many of the projective personality tests are widely used, only a few people are recognized as truly competent to interpret them, even for clinical purposes. What is equally important, the interpretation is not an objective process, but a function of the tester's theoretical background and assumptions.[8] We are not dealing with simple measurements of simple qualities but with complex interpretations, based in part on the theoretical bias and personal projection of the psychologist. Even if we grant that the company has a right to invade the psychic privacy of the individual, we can still ask if it has the right to expose the individual to evaluation at the hands of someone whose tools are not truly objective, and are subject to serious doubt by professional colleagues.

Then again, there is serious doubt about the value of projective tests as predictors of success in a business situation. Thus, the Rorschack, or ink blot test, though it is one of the most widely used, "also has a longer history of inconclusive and contradictory findings than any other test."[9] According to Gellerman, the Rorschack, the Bernreuter Personality Inventory and the A.S. Reaction Study have at best given indifferent results in predicting vocational success or failure.[10] Among other reasons for this is that people, jobs, companies and work environment are so different that it is almost impossible to say how a given personality will react in a complex, unforeseeable situation. The question arises, then, as to whether or not a company has a right to use its stockholders' money for such programs?

It should be noted that there are similar objections to various personality inventories. Ellis notes that since the tests are long and hard to score, "It is to be wondered whether the clinical psychologist who cannot in equal or less time, get more pertinent, incisive, and depth-centered 'personality' material from a straightforward interview technique, is worth his salt."[11] Others have observed that they have had their greatest success with tests which consisted largely of personal history, background, or biographical interest items.[12] All this would tend to suggest that there has been a great deal of unethical selling of magic tests to business.

As we have already noted, there is nothing surprising about this. Tests and inventories may help to weed out obvious misfits, but the situation of an employee is so individual and so changeable, that it is almost impossible to predict how he will react. This is all the truer since the reaction is affected by the other people with whom he works, not only by the job itself. For this reason, professional psychologists are wary when working in business: there is no general population of general managers from which to derive criteria for company X.

These remarks are not to be taken as an attack on the utility of these tests in truly clinical situations. The problem arises in business, and from the application of the tests to a situation for which they were not designed. However, even in the clinical area the behavioral implications of these methods are not clear.[14] The clinicians believe that it may be a grave error to predict from fantasy to reality behavior, since we do not know how the various factors interact to produce behavior.[15]

Strangely enough some companies have found that individuals who are emotionally unstable and insecure may make very fine executives.[16] The creative, offbeat personality may be the one needed for top executive positions which involve breaking new ground rather than adjusting to one's environment.

A final set of problems arises from the fact that the tests are given in a setting that is neither clinical, therapeutic nor proper to scientific research. While the psychologist is hired by the company for the good of the company, he must still protect those relationships with his subjects that are necessary for the good of the profession and for the welfare of clients: and those relationships belong in a truly clinical setting. Here we meet the problems of professional secrecy, reporting, and recommending.

The Right to Privacy

In the ordinary clinical or research setting, the patient has voluntarily consented to reveal his personality to the psychologist. Except in certain extreme cases, there is seldom any question of a violation of privacy in these situations.[17] In business, on the other hand, the employee is being forced to undergo the test as part of the price of being hired, placed or promoted. Even here, of course, there is no problem when the tests merely ascertain characteristics manifested by ordinary speech and behavior: these are hardly the object of the right to privacy. Difficulties present themselves when the test seeks to explore such deeper levels as sexual identification, oral eroticism and so forth.

Even if information about such matters were useful for the purposes of commercial placement, it lies beyond the rightful domain of any third party. To ask a man to reveal such points, whether directly or indirectly, and for purely commercial motives, is to ask him not merely to sell his labor, but the inner secrets of his being. If this inner sphere of defect, weakness and feeling, this area of suppressed and controlled drives, is not private and even sacred, then the right to privacy is completely meaningless. We cannot use another's body at will; much less can we use his mind—especially in the mere pursuit of gain. We cannot force ourselves into a man's home without just and sufficient reason, nor can we penetrate the inner castle of his soul for motives of profit.

There may be cases where there is reason for probing more deeply into a personality, but in general any such attempt—

without the truly free consent of the subject—could be considered a violation of both liberty and personal dignity.[18] This point needs to be stressed since, once the line is crossed, there is a temptation to use man as a thing and to subject him to the corporation and society even in the intimate sphere of his personality. If we do not maintain high principles in this area, we shall run the risk of subjecting men not only to tests but to brainwashing, in the name of business and the community.

The projective tests pose a peculiar problem since, at least in theory, they are supposed to throw light on overt characteristics too, in which case there is no question of the inner world being penetrated. Since these areas of valid information can be reached by techniques which do not in any way enter the intimate sphere, it does not seem right to ask the subject to expose himself even *indirectly* to a violation of his rights by more probing tests.

We must stress that the question is quite different when the tests are performed for therapeutic purposes. In these cases, the consent is, or should be, free, and the subject is protected by professional secrecy and justified in consenting by the proportionate good to be obtained by revealing his inner secrets. So too, in a pure research situation where the subject consents freely and where his name or identification is not used, we are not dealing with a violation of the inner sphere. In a commercial sphere, where the test is imposed primarily for the good of the company, the intervention seems unjustified.

Right of the Company to Information

This is not to deny that the company has a right to certain information about its employees. Information is necessary for the proper functioning of the organization, and the company has a right to it. But this right is limited not only by the pre-existent rights of the employee but also by the needs of the company and by the relevance of the information. The right does not extend to information that *might* be useful but to information that is, as Gellerman has put it, "directly relevant to the probable work performance of the testee, or that which will help management in developing him."[19]

Since what we know of the personality tests indicates that they have little predictive value as to behavior, we can conclude that management has no right to use them, even if they did not involve a violation of privacy. Such tests are needlessly inquisitive and superfluous. Indeed, we can also conclude that on the whole they are wasteful, for purposes of placement and promotion.

Management has other legitimate means of getting relevant information, not the least of which is the straight interview by a trained man. Management also has access to tests of mental ability, of interests and knowledge of the field, which can be used as a supplement to analysis of past experience, planned interviews and appraisal by associates.[20] We might note however, that even when only these means are used, management has a real responsibility not to dodge responsibility by appeal to nice, neat cut-off figures on test scores. As any psychologist or consulting management firm will insist, these are only supplements to traditional and basic evaluation procedures.

The use of the lie detector, or polygraph, poses some similar problems. There are, however, at least two important differences. First, the lie detector is not used to probe the innermost depths of the person. Second, there appear to be cases where it is the only way of making sure of information which is of real importance not only to the company but to the employee and society. One transport company for example, uses them to detect alcoholics who apply for jobs as drivers.[21] A large drug firm uses them to detect addicts among people who will have access to legally restricted drugs. In such cases, it would appear that the company has a right to use the lie detector. Here as elsewhere, however, the need for such testing should be established rather than assumed.

The Utility of Testing

Because an executive has an obligation to work for the good of the company as well as to respect the privacy of employees, it is necessary to evaluate the utility of testing from a business point of view. This is all the more necessary because there is some evidence that managers have used the tests to escape making decisions, or as a defense when they have made mistakes in selecting personnel. This is true of aptitude and achievement tests as well as of personality inventories.

As we have said, the predictive value of personality tests is low. However, some tests provide leads for intensive interviews when the score is low, though not when it is high.[22] The tests which do provide valuable leads generally require a high degree of specialized training for proper administration and use. Other tests can be fudged and are, so, less than useless. Self-evaluating tests can be faked and a reliance on them can do injustice to both the individual who takes them and to the company.[23] In any event, tests of any sort should only be used as one piece of information so that selection and promotion should never be based on test scores alone.

Scepticism seems to be a necessary virtue in these areas, for even skilled personnel men have been deceived.[24] Dr. Ross Stagner of Wayne State University administered an experimental test to a group at a conference of personnel managers. The professor gave each manager the same vaguely written report as the results of his individual test. Though all items were the same on all reports, 50% evaluated the report as being an amazingly correct evaluation of their own personality, while another 40%

thought it was at least a good picture of themselves.[25] This despite the professor's specific warning to be careful in evaluating the report.

In any event, management should be aware that even the best of tests, administered by the best of psychologists, may arouse hostility in employees who are afraid of being manipulated. Sometimes, it is better to omit even a technically valuable procedure than to destroy or weaken morale.

Reporting

In a clinical or research situation, the psychologist is bound by clearly defined rules of professional secrecy. In the business world, when acting as a consultant, his situation is somewhat ambiguous. The *Ethical Standards of Psychologists,* put out by the American Psychological Association, has the following provisions:

Principle 2.24-2 Information obtained in clinical or consulting relationships should be discussed only in professional meetings and with professional persons clearly concerned with the case.

Principle 2.24-3 In clinical and consulting situations where possible division of loyalties exists, as between a client and the employer of the psychologist, agreement concerning the handling of confidential materials must be worked out and the nature of the agreement made known to all concerned. (cf Principle 2.13-1)

Principle 2.24-4 When the psychologist's position is such that some departure is required from the normal expectation that clinical or consulting relationships are confidential, it is expected that the psychologist will make clear to the client the nature of his role before the client enters into the relationship. (cf Principle 2.31-1, 2.21-2, 6.21-1)

Principle 2.21-1 A cardinal obligation of the clinical or consulting psychologist is to respect the integrity and protect the welfare of the person with whom he is working. Vigilant regard for this principle should characterize all of the work of the psychologist and pervade all his professional relationships.

Principle 2.21-2 Clinical services must not be imposed upon an individual, nor should a person be unduly urged to avail himself of such services.

Granted that a person has been forced into a consulting relationship, the psychologist must keep these general points in mind. In addition, even when the data is not concerned with the innermost sphere, the following particular points should be observed.[26]

Ordinarily only a recommendation should be turned over to management. There are two reasons for this. First, unless the manager has some training he will not be able to use specific data correctly and fairly. Secondly, the necessity of protecting the good name of the profession demands that publication of personal data be held to the minimum. If a justification of the recommendation is required, it should be presented in such a way that no false conclusions can be drawn.[27] Technical language, though accurate, can be deceptive to the layman, and such factors must be considered if the report is to be fair to all involved.

In this connection, the psychologist must be careful to present his recommendations as professional opinion rather than fact, and to avoid giving an impression of absoluteness and finality.[28] The report must stress this aspect since management may be tempted to skip the subtle qualifications and discover a fact where none exists.

For similar reasons, both the company and the psychologist are obliged to restrict the number of people who have access to the data. Test papers should be destroyed when an employee leaves the company, lest they fall into the hands of unauthorized personnel. Further, the tests are not to be shown to anyone except the qualified personnel of the company for which the original work was done. Exceptions may be made only when the testee gives written permission to use the results.

Though most of these latter obligations fall primarily on the psychologists, they imply certain duties on the part of management. First, management has an obligation to provide for the proper safeguarding and subsequent destruction of test results. Secondly, management should not seek access to material which is professional unless the managers are competent to interpret it on their own. Thirdly, management has a serious obligation to check the competence and integrity of those who administer and interpret tests. Unless this is done, management can certainly not act on recommendations made by psychologists.

It is necessary to remember that the existence of even valid and reliable tests does not excuse the manager from making his own decisions. Above all, he must remember that his employees do have rights and that the mere fact that a procedure is effective does not justify its use in business.

Notes

1. William H. Whyte, Jr., *The Organization Man* (Simon and Schuster, 1956), chapter 15 and Appendix, "How to Cheat on Personality Tests."
2. *Cf.* Lewis B. Ward, "Problems in Review: Putting Executives to the Test," *Harvard Business Review,* July-August, 1960 (vol. 38, no. 4), pp. 6-7; 10-15; 164 ff.
3. *Ibid.,* p. 10.
4. *Ibid.,* p. 175.
5. *Ethical Standards for Psychologists* (The American Psychological Association, 1953).
6. Saul W. Gellerman, "The Ethics of Personality Testing," *Personnel,* November-December, 1958, pp. 30-35.
7. "Lie Detectors: When Does It Make Sense to Use a Polygraph

Test for Employment?" *Employment Relations Bulletin,* December 13, 1961, Report no. 788.

8. Morris I. Stern, *The Thematic Apperception Test* (Cambridge, Mass.: Addison Wesley, 1955), p. 77.

9. Robert M. Allen, *Personality Assessment Procedures* (Harper and Brothers, 1958), pp. 159 ff.

10. Frederich Gehlmann *et al., Personality Tests: Uses and Limitations* (Personnel Report no. 561, Civil Service Assembly, 1956), p. 9.

11. Albert Ellis, "Minnesota Multiphasic Personality Inventory: Revised Edition," in Oscar Krisen Buros (ed.), *The Fifth Mental Measurements Yearbook* (Highland Park, N.J.: Gryphon Press, 1959), p. 167.

12. Gehlmann, *op. cit.,* p. 7.

13. Gerthe Williams and Samuel Kellman, "The Rorschack Technique in Industrial Psychology," in Bruno Klopfer (ed.), *Developments in the Rorschack Technique* (Yonkers, N.Y.: World Book Company, 1954), vol. ii, p. 589.

14. Mary D. Ainsworth, "Problems in Validation," in Bruno Klopfer, *op. cit.,* vol. i, p. 489.

15. *Ibid.,* p. 490.

16. "Maverick Managers," *The Wall Street Journal,* Wednesday, November 22, 1961, pp. 1 and 23.

17. Even in the clinical situation it is assumed that the revelation is free and does not extend beyond the area where clinical help is important.

18. G. Perico, S.J., "Il segreto professionale," *Aggiornamenti Sociali,* November, 1960 (vol. xi, no. 11), p. 581.

19. Gellerman, *op. cit.,* p. 33.

20. *Cf. Management Appraisal-Key to Building Executives* (New York: Booz, Allen and Hamilton, N.D.).

21. *Cf.* note 7 *supra.*

22. *G. E. Personnel Selection Program, Part II* (N.D.), p. 43. It is interesting to note that only one page out of sixty is devoted to personality testing.

23. Harold E. Yuhar and J. R. Block, "Common Sense about Psychological Tests," *Personnel,* May-June, 1960, p. 48.

24. Daniel M. Goodacre, III, "Pitfalls in the Use of Psychological Tests," *Personnel*, March-April, 1958.
25. *Cf.* Ross Stagner, "The Gullibility of Personnel Managers," *Personnel Psychology*, August, 1958 (vol. 11, no. 3), pp. 347-352.
26. *Cf.* Wendell L. French, "What Every Executive Should Know About Psychological Testing," *Personnel Journal*, February, 1961 (vol. 39, no. 9), pp. 351-355, 377 ff.
27. Walter Klopfer, "Principles of Reporting Writing," in Bruno Klopfer (ed.), *op. cit.*, vol. i, p. 602.
28. Harry Levinson, "The Psychologist in Industry," *Harvard Business Review*, September-October, 1959 (vol. 37, no. 5), p. 96.

8 THE COMPUTER AND EXECUTIVE DECISION

Introduction

THE INTRODUCTION OF NEW METHODS into business generally raises ethical as well as technical questions. Frequently, however, the ethical aftermath is overlooked because management is fully occupied with problems of efficiency. This was true in the case of psychological testing. It would appear to be true in that area of business where the giant computer has begun to exercise its influence on management decisions.

As yet, there is no catalogue of problems which may arise, but the nature of both the computer and management decisions concerning it give some hints as to what may be expected. If the aftermaths of automation in the factory are any indication, the problems posed by the computer in the office and board room may be among the gravest facing, not only business, but government and society as a whole.[1]

Computers, along with other office machines, are already handling payrolls, accounting, market research, budget and operating forecasts, production scheduling and inventory control. There is, indeed, more use of such automated processes in the office than in the factory.[2]

All this is impressive, but it may make us forget that we are dealing not merely with a gadget or a technological innovation, but with a way of thinking.[3] It is the nature and limits of this way of thinking that have alarmed such experts as Norbert Weiner,[4] and C. P. Snow.[5] To appreciate their anxiety, it is necessary to have some idea of the machine's intrinsic limits and of the way in which its "thought" differs from that of man.

The Computers[6]

Essentially, the computer is a machine that records numbers, operates with numbers, and gives answers in numerical form.[7] Some of the machines now have receptors which enable them to get new information, memories which store it, and even a sort of nervous system by which they can check their own operation. The very latest models are constructed to "learn" from previous mistakes, and to modify their operational instructions.[8] For all this, they remain, in the last analysis, machines which deal with numbers, or at least with relationships expressed in a quantified way and according to the rules of a mathematical logic.

In the case of the digital computer, the type most commonly used, the data is represented as a set of choices among a number of contingencies. The accuracy of the machine depends, quite obviously, on the sharpness with which the contingencies have been distinguished, and on the number of alternatives given. Generally, the machines operate on a system of binary choices, that is of questions which can be answered by a yes or no; though they can, by the use of a special logic, be programmed to include a "don't know" reply.

Though the machine can make choices on the basis of the information put into it, it is man who picks the goal to be attained. At best the machine is like a pilot who receives his orders from the captain of the ship and then relays them to the engine room and to the steersman. If the goal has been improperly chosen, carelessly defined, or even changed, the machine will grind out answers which, though they may be logical in terms of the instructions given it, may be at odds with the actual purpose of the captain. The machine can, in other words, be like the logical paranoiac, who is perfectly consistent with his premises, but completely out of contact with the real world.

In addition, it is the captain who decides which factors the machine is to consider in guiding the ship. If he has omitted some point of importance, the answer given will be incomplete. From one point of view, the captain is always omitting some information. Since the machine can only handle numbers and formalized thought, the captain must speak to it in a language which has been simplified so that it does not convey all aspects of reality. Simplifications can be useful and legitimate, but they can also be dangerous when you are dealing with man, that most complex of all creatures.

In practice, the use of machines can involve not one but many simplifications. Let us suppose that the machine is to be programmed so as to help in the selection of executives. First, the selector must decide which factors are significant for his purposes. Second, he must decide on the relative importance of each factor, so that it can be weighed. Now, since emotional balance, motivation, initiative, intelligence, skill, vision and general character cannot be measured directly, he must decide which things are generally, though not necessarily, signs of these interior qualities. Each of these signs must then be given a weight and fitted to an equation. These last two steps also involve a set of assumptions. The statistical work which determined the original correlations between the signs and the character traits depended on a psychological as well as a statistical theory. Finally, since the equation itself may be selected on the basis of its ability to give results in accord with the theory, another simplification is necessary.

The nature of the simplifications and theorizing that go into the programming of a computer is such that its answers are unintelligible except to someone who understands the background of the process. The amateur who sees only the neat answer may forget that a statistical probability refers to groups and cannot be applied to individuals. Even an intelligent person might think the answer an irrefutable conclusion, whereas it is only an opinion based on theory as well as on selected facts. In other words, since a conclusion is no better than its antecedents, its meaning can be fully understood only by those who know the premises from which it came.

The difficulty of understanding is increased when the computer is able to modify its own program, or takes in data through its own receptors.[9] Unless the user can check on these modifications, he may have no idea of certain significant factors. This can be a crucial problem, for when the computer's results are to be made a part of a human decision, it is necessary to know whether or not they are built on sound human principles.

Human Thought and the Computer

Machine "thought", then, differs from human thought. And because business decisions will take place at the point where the two modes of thinking meet, a knowledge of both is necessary if the union is to be fruitful and without danger.

Human thought is the operation of a living totality. It begins and ends in a man who not only senses, knows, reacts, but loves and hates and sympathizes, with other men. Sometimes human knowing is discursive, sometimes intuitive. Most often, it appears to be conscious and discursive, but may be instinctive, poetic, more feeling than reasoning. Man, moreover, though he can and, generally, should be logical, knows when logic will lead to ridiculous conclusions. In time, man even learns to accept and live with contradictions. Laughter, one of the most distinctive human acts, seems to spring from the recognition of a contradiction. Unlike the machine, which needs clear-cut distinctions, the human mind can and does operate with ambiguous ideas.

Human thought develops from a complex interaction between various minds, each of which grasps some aspect of reality which the others have missed. This means that true human thought is subject to a system of checks and balances, in most cases. Moreover, because the interaction is between persons, and not merely between disembodied intellects, human thought is enriched by all the subtle, inexpressible nuances of individual differences and social values. We do not always enjoy a real understanding of this process, but we recognize its importance. Indeed, our intuitions and hunches, while not very scientific, are generally appreciated as being of prime importance in the decisions we make.

Hunch and intuition play an important part in business and should not be overlooked. Even after elaborate credit checks, the decisive factor in making a loan is often the character of the applicant. Computers can help in assembling data in investment work, but it is the evaluation of management's ability that generally tips the scale one way or another.

Computers, obviously, are quite different from the human mind. They operate in a hygienic world of logic and in terms of clear-cut alternatives. Their operations have been purified of love, hate, feeling and sympathy. Their knowledge has been filtered until the individual, the ineffable and the personal, have disappeared. Computer "thought" is depersonalized thought. It is not human.[10] Indeed, where the machine is capable of modifying its own instructions, it is hard to say if the "thinking" of one computer is like that of its brothers and sisters.

Machine thinking starts with what men have put into it and, in most cases, follows the rules which have been given by men. The results of the machine's work also enter into the world of men. In between, however, there is none of that complex human interaction which gives human thought a good deal of its truly human warmth and subtilty. In theory, such an interaction should precede the programming and follow the receipt of the answer.[11] But in practice, this interaction may be seriously impaired, since only a limited number of men speak the machine's language. This, plus the numerous simplifications necessary to program the machine in the first place, means that machine thought is truly depersonalized. This is one of its merits, but it is also one of its shortcomings. For this reason, Postley writes:

Furthermore, it is not entirely impossible that presently unforeseen factors (probably human) will limit the operational employment of decision making to an extent far greater than its advocates now believe.[12]

Interviews with programmers indicate that these difficulties are not merely possible, but real. While the computer experts insist that those who are to use the machine must work with the programmers, it is difficult to make sure that the program reflects the directions and desires of all in the chain of command. As a result, the solutions proposed by the computer are often discarded by middle management because it knows that they will not fit in with the thinking of top management. One wonders, however, if the top executive would reject a computer decision because it did not fit in with the thinking of those who must execute it.

There is one other aspect in which computer thinking and human thinking may be vastly different. Both men and computers solve problems, but, so far as we know, the human mind alone can frame a problem. This is important, for unless a man asks the right question, the machine's answer, even if right, will be useless.[13] Which means that man must still bear the responsibility for the questions he asks and for the problems he formulates.

Postley feels that the major difficulty may be in making sure that the mathematical terms actually reflect the *real* problem.[14] He gives five reasons for this. First, the man who knows the mathematics usually does not know the basic nature of the undefined problems he encounters. Second, the people who have the problems are often without an airtight logical definition of them. Third, nonmathematical or human considerations are often present, and sometimes dominate the solution. Fourth, the data used to develop the equations intended to define the decision, often fail to constitute a representative sample of the total information generated. Fifth, the data used for the solution may be incomplete and/or inaccurately gathered.

Uses and Dangers

Despite all the limitations mentioned in the previous pages, there is no doubt that the computer has a vast range of legitimate uses. It can be substituted for man in a large number of routine tasks which involve working with numbers and making decisions on the basis of numbers or patterns. Though this replacement of man by the machine does cause temporary disturbances in employment, it should, in the long run, free human energies for more significant tasks.

Because the machine can handle more data than a man, and handle it more rapidly, it can, in areas of routine, numerical tasks, lead to a better and more efficient use of time. Indeed, if it presents the human decision maker with better data, it can probably improve the quality of human decisions, and possibly of decision making itself. The very fact that the programming of a computer demands a precise formulation of problems and an analysis of alternative solutions, may force humans to rethink their ways of acting. At the same time, the impact of the machine on human thinking gives rise to difficulties and potential abuses.

The machines force men to think out problems in terms understandable to the machine. As the assembly line tended to force its rhythm on the worker, the computer tends to impose its nature on the user. This poses no difficulty in regard to routine and numerically solvable problems. When the problems are in an area heavy with human involvement, of major policy decisions or of intuitive grasp of complex human social situations, there is real danger.

There is, as one writer has noted, a danger that the use of machines can change the deadly problem of war, or a crucial business decision, into a challenge or a game.[15] In this context, Norbert Wiener comments as follows:

If the rules for victory in a war game, do not correspond to what we actually wish for our country, it is more likely that such a machine may produce a policy that will win a nominal victory on points at the cost of every interest we have at heart, even that of national survival.[16]

This danger arises from several factors. First, the use of the machine can isolate us from the real meaning of what we are doing.[17] That is to say, we may think that we are dealing only with numbers, and forget that they represent men. Secondly, as Wiener has noted in his article on *Some Moral and Technical Consequences of Automation*:[18]

It may be seen that the result of a programming technique of (cybernation) is to remove from the mind of the designer and operator an effective understanding of many of the stages by which the machine comes to its conclusions and of what the real tactical intentions of many of its operations may be. This is highly relevant to the problem of our being able to foresee undesired consequences outside the frame of the strategy of the game while the machine is still in action and while intervention on our part may prevent the occurrence of these consequences. Here it is necessary to realize that human action is a feedback action. To avoid a disastrous consequence, it is not enough that some action on our part should be sufficient to change the course of the machine, because it is quite possible that we lack information on which to base consideration of such an action.

This difficulty would exist in any use of the computer, but it is particularly great when the computer is used in making decisions about means to truly human ends. The goals of men, at least their ultimate goals, can not generally be expressed mathematically. Among other things, men generally have several subgoals whose interrelation shifts in time, so that it is hard to anticipate the configuration of all goals at a future date.[19] If the machine tempts a man to commit himself to one set of goals in one configuration the result may be a disastrous rigidity—especially disastrous in areas where flexibility is of the essence.

The temptation to commit oneself to a rigid set of sub-goals can be strong, for the machine, with its neat, clear answers, gives the appearance of rationality. Unfortunately, clarity and logical consistency are not enough. Human decision-making demands that men test goals, means, and the interrelation of the two, for ethical relevance. Such testing almost invariably involves ambiguity and the vast, murky grey areas which have appeared so often in earlier chapters.

For the sake of illustration, suppose that the programmer has not included social and human costs such as water pollution or worker health, in their calculations of the profitability of an operation. (Most economic theory makes no allowances for such factors.) With these costs omitted from the program, the answer may be correct from the narrow view point of the firm, and immoral from a social and human standpoint. If the executive who uses the results is fully aware of the omission, he can adjust. If he has no such awareness, he may feel justified in acting, since he has a clear-cut mathematical decision to support him. Similarly, if a program for executive selection omits such qualities as a sense of social responsibility and vision, the machine may recommend men who are ruthless and narrow.

In short, the computer can be dangerous unless those who program it and those who use it have a sound social sense and an awareness of the limitations of the machine. In practice it may be difficult to maintain this awareness, for Americans have a great reverence for the gadget and a mysterious awe of the skilled technician who is master of it. As C. P. Snow has noted:

People get fascinated by gadgets. They love them. They want everything to be explained in terms of their gadget. They think it is the answer to everything on heaven and earth. All the bad decisions I have seen have some element of gadgetry in them.[20]

This is not merely the reaction of a naive ethician. Several authors have noted that management has not only been fascinated, but also intimidated, by the extreme complexity of automation. In some cases, they have allowed the technicians to take over not only the operation of the machines, but also the management decisions as to how they are to be used. Others have noted a tendency on the part of some executives to buy high-priced scientific services to use as excuses in the event of failures.

As automation increases, the influence of the engineers will rise.[21] Given that technicians are more interested in efficiency than in human values, there is a danger that the latter may be relegated to second place. The combination of executive ignorance or irresponsibility, and engineering rationality, may produce a basically amoral climate of decision.

Though the machines will not take over the world, the very decision to use them in human areas poses these problems. Because I must select factors which can be expressed mathematically, I am tempted to omit those which will not fit my requirements, and to distort others in an effort to make them fit. The need for quantification may lead to a stripping off of the nonquantifiable layers of reality and to reducing man to a cipher. The demands of the machine can thus re-create the creator to the image and likeness of his creature.

While this last point may seem extreme, those who have had even a little experience with such relatively simple machines as those used to work out college schedules and teacher programs will see the danger. Because the machine can take only a certain kind of data, and because the programming becomes more expensive as the number of factors is increased, there is a temptation to tailor the data—that is, in the case of colleges, the faculty—to the machine. Further, since changes are expensive and time consuming, there is also great hesitancy about remodeling the straightjacket once it has been cut to size. For example, sensible scheduling should consider the health of the professor, his energy pattern, the number of preparations, and even his distance from school. Now, though the machine could consider many of these factors, it cannot do so without increased expense. If an administrator leaves these out of consideration, he may find himself with a very unhappy faculty.

It is for reasons of this sort that the experts insist on comprehension of the human element when automation of any sort is installed.[22] It would, after all, be irrational to expect humans to act in accord with the logic of a machine which lacks feelings and real individuality. Unfortunately, the administrator may think otherwise and consider himself freed from the duty of dealing with people.

The experts insist that the computers, though they can make some simple decisions between clear-cut alternatives, cannot exercise that subtle and complex human judgment which is the essence of real management. The automated office may be an aid to management, but it cannot substitute for real managerial responsibility. As a matter of fact, the computers may even increase this responsibility since the need for human relations increases as the demands of routine work decline.

The manager must be on his guard about this. According to Hoos, the "failure to recognize the workers' point of view typifies most of the Electric Data Processing executives in firms" she has studied.[23] As a result the EDP department is sometimes found encroaching on the personnel and industrial relations sections. This could be disastrous. Although the machines may have filtered out much of the human interaction necessary to truly human thought, the personnel and industrial relations managers are still capable of restoring it: but only if they have retained their own independence.

Above all, the executive must remember that gadgets are not substitutes for creative business imagination.[24] The art of top management decision eludes routine formulae. The problems of top management are more often than not concerned with once-in-a-lifetime situations, for which there are few if any guides. The use of computers cannot help the executive to escape from the terrible task of decision making.

The Computer in Government[25]

Before attempting to list the major obligations connected with computers, we should note that many of them must be faced not only by business but by government. Indeed, the computer in government may pose a very special difficulty.

C. P. Snow, who has experience as both a scientist and administrator, sees a new form of secret government growing up around the computer. Already there is a type of secret government, with scientists who know the facts, and politicians who must make the decisions, at the center. Snow sees the possibility that we will end up with a small circle of computer experts, a larger circle of scientists who are not familiar with the decision-making rules, and finally the outer circle of politicians and administrators. While admitting that you can build-in rules to make computer judgment defer to human judgment, Sir Charles suspects that the man next to the machine is going to be excessively influential. Because of the nature of these people he writes:

And I suspect that computers in government are going to get into the hands of persons with mildly defective or canalized judgment and become gadgets. It will be astounding if this does not happen.[26]

Such a movement would reduce effective democracy and remove even elected representatives from the center of decision. It might even constitute a grave danger to freedom, since the smaller the centers of power, the easier it is to grasp them. Thus, the problem of the computer should concern all who are interested not only in efficient business but in the preservation of freedom.

Obligations

Though the evidence and opinions presented will not warrant a long catalogue of obligations, they will permit us to affirm certain broad duties. In the first place, the calculator must always be treated as an aid to, and not a substitute for, personal decision. A failure in this point may lead to a further weakening of the sense of responsibility, if not to outright disaster.

Since a proper evaluation of the results given by a machine depends on an understanding of its program, goal, limits and even philosophy, there is a real obligation to study these matters. The general obligation to be technically competent now includes a duty to understand the new tools available to management.[27] Obviously, the professors of business and of social ethics, who are training the future executives, should introduce their students to this type of problem. Unless we can form men who are at once technically competent and humanistically oriented, there will be no possibility of integrating the computer and other scientific advances into human life, and it is likely that man will be trimmed to fit the machine.

This educational task cannot be accomplished merely by adding more courses to the curriculum. Nor can it be achieved by dovetailing the existing courses. The need to integrate social and ethical considerations into decision making requires a broader view of economics, sociology and political science: without it, the new mathematical tools will only increase the old problems.

The businessman who is going to work with the new instruments must above all avoid the temptation to use them as escapes from responsibility. No matter how precise his mathematical answers may be, he must always remember that he is dealing with men, whose reactions are far more important than mere technical considerations. The businessman must realize that he cannot understand the computer's answers unless he has participated in framing the questions, checking the program, and interpreting the whole process in terms of human impact.

To repeat: the real thinking and decision making is still done by the men involved in the process. This seems to indicate that as we are freed from the boredom of routine, we must face more and more the fundamental human problems of business society. This need not surprise us, for each addition to our effective freedom increases the burden of anxiety and makes us more aware that, however much we may conquer nature, self-mastery and the realization of our true destiny are the ultimate tasks. No machine can liberate us from this obligation, however much danger there is that it might cause us to forget it.[28]

Notes

1. *Cf.* Francis Quinn, S.J. (ed.), *The Ethical Aftermath of Automation* (Westminster, Maryland: Newman, 1962). Most of this book is devoted to the impact of automation on employment. My own contribution, of which the present chapter is an expansion, is the only one that treats of the decision making aspect.
2. Walter Buckingham, *Automation: Its Impact on Business and People* (Harper and Brothers, 1961), p. 50.
3. John Diebold, *Automation: Its Impact on Business and Labor* (National Planning Association, May, 1959), p. 3, cited by Donald Michael, *Cybernation: The Silent Conquest* (Center for the Study of Democratic Institutions, 1962), p. 5.
4. Norbert Wiener, "Some Moral and Technical Consequences of Automation," *Science,* May 6, 1960 (vol. 131, no. 3410), cited by Michael, *op. cit.,* p. 8.
5. C. P. Snow, "Scientists and Decision Making," in Martin Greenberger (ed.), *Management and the Computer of the Future* (Cambridge, Mass.: Technology Press, 1962), pp. 3-13.
6. I have used the following books in preparing this description: Norbert Wiener, *Cybernetics* (John Wiley, 1948) and *The Human Use of Human Beings* (2nd ed., Doubleday, 1954); G. T. Guibaud, *What Is Cybernetics?* trans. by V. Mackay (New York: Criterion Books, 1959) and Irving Adler, *Thinking Machines* (John Day, 1961).
7. Wiener, *Cybernetics,* p. 136.
8. Michael, *op. cit.,* pp. 8-9 and a questioner in Greenberger, *op. cit.,* pp. 127-128.
9. *Loc. cit.*
10. Carl Dreher, *Automation* (W. W. Norton, 1957), p. 75.
11. John A. Postley, *Computers and People* (McGraw-Hill, 1960), p. 114.
12. *Ibid.,* p. 119.
13. Elton E. Morison, comments in Greenberger, *op. cit.,* p. 16, and Peter F. Drucker, *The Practice of Management* (Harper and Brothers, 1954), pp. 352-353.
14. Postley, *op. cit.,* p. 97; *cf.* Irwin D. J. Bross, "Looking Around:

Statistical Decision Making," *Harvard Business Review*, September-October, 1954 (vol. 32, no. 5), p. 142, for some interesting remarks on the dangers of applying game theory to business.

15. Albert Baylis, "The Dehumanizing Effect of the Computer," in *Computers and Automation*, August, 1961 (vol. 10, no. 8), p. 8.

16. Norbert Wiener, cited in *Time*, January 11, 1960.

17. Baylis, *op. cit.*, p. 26.

18. Wiener, "Some Moral and Technical Consequences of Automation," cited in Michael, *op. cit.*, p. 9.

19. *Cf.* remarks of Marvin L. Minsky in Greenberger, *op. cit.*, p. 117.

20. C. P. Snow, *op. cit.*, p. 12.

21. Frederich Pollack, *Automation: A Study of Its Economic and Social Consequences* (New York: Praeger, 1957), p. 227.

22. Buckingham, *op. cit.*, p. 63 and Pollack, *op. cit.*, p. 223.

23. Ida Russakoff Hoos, "When the Computer Takes Over the Office," *Harvard Business Review*, July-August, 1960 (vol. 38, no. 4), p. 109.

24. *Cf.* David McCord Wright, "The Administrative Fallacy," *Harvard Business Review*, July-August, 1960 (vol. 38, no. 4), pp. 113-114, and Melvin Anshen, "The Manager and the Black Box," *Harvard Business Review*, November-December, 1960 (vol. 38, no. 6), pp. 85-92, especially p. 89.

25. My remarks are merely a paraphrase of those of C. P. Snow, *op. cit.*, pp. 10-13.

26. *Ibid.*, p. 12.

27. Buckingham, *op. cit.*, p. 64 and Alexander Henderson and Robert Schlaifer, "Mathematical Programming: Better Information for Better Decision Making," *Harvard Business Review*, May-June, 1957 (vol. 32), p. 94.

28. Paul Einzig, *The Economic Consequences of Automation* (W. W. Norton, 1957), p. 246.

9 BUSINESS POWER OVER PUBLIC OPINION

Introduction[1]

MUCH CRITICISM OF BUSINESS springs from a fear of its alleged power not only over the economy and government, but over the root of power, public opinion. This fear is all the greater because we have supposed things to be the other way around: the public consensus, and the public opinion to which it gives rise, is supposed to control and guide the corporation, even in the absence of specific government regulation.[2] If business can control opinion, the consumer is no longer king and democracy has given way to an oligarchy of those who can purchase the opinion makers' services. What, however, are the facts? Can businessmen, or any other private group, control public opinion? If so, what is the extent of its power, and its responsibility?

At the very start, it must be admitted that scientists do not know a great deal about how public opinion is formed, controlled and guided. What little we do know indicates that common sense and common prejudices are of little help. It is still necessary to use the meager information available to form even a tentative judgment of the power and responsibility of business in the sphere of opinion formation.

Brainwashing[3]

Let us start our consideration with the most awesome and seemingly most successful of all techniques for changing the opinions of men: brainwashing. Two notes are in order. First, the older brainwashing techniques which involved torture and mistreatment of prisoners have to a large extent been replaced by more subtle techniques of "education." The communists in Korea, for example, used regular classes and group discussion rather than outright violence. Secondly even the best brainwashing techniques are not uniformly successful. Thus, though the Americans in Korea had a very poor record of resistance, the Turks resisted to a man.

Communist brainwashing, as practiced in Korea and in the Iron Curtain countries, implies a complete control of all formal means of communication and of living conditions, and at least the capability of inflicting severe punishments. This is an important condition for success and, since it cannot be duplicated in the free nations of the world, we need not fear the full impact of the techniques, unless we have already lost the basic freedoms. Furthermore, those who have studied the failure of American soldiers to resist, note that the techniques worked only when there was a lack of leadership and social cohesion, and principally on those men who had no internalized values. The communists could operate effectively only when normal social controls had broken down and each man sought only his own comfort. As a rule the technique was most successful with those men whose brains were already blank sheets of paper. This too is an important consideration since it indicates that the greatest danger arises only when the opinion maker has a social and moral vacuum into which he can pour his ideas.

While there can be no doubt that the brainwashing changed many minds during the time when the soldiers were actually in the prison camps, it is also true that these effects were not, on the whole, permanent. When the victims were freed and re-stored to their homes, they generally returned to their regular ways of thinking. In only a few cases were any observable and permanent results achieved. It would appear, then, that even under ideal circumstances, brainwashing is not an all-powerful technique.

Totalitarian propaganda, like brainwashing, seems to depend for its success on the existence of similar conditions in both the society and the individual. Hitler, for example, came to power in a demoralized Germany where the people longed for a strong leader to give them security and a new national pride. The First World War, the Treaty of Versailles, the inflation of the twenties, and the collapse of the traditional leadership, created a chaos into which "the strong man" could step. In the second place, Hitler did not depend on mass communication techniques so much as on group formation, pageants, activities, and on the careful organization of all those who wished to discharge their violence on society.[4]

Our recent experiences with the totalitarian propaganda of the Russians also indicates that even control of the press, the radio and the schools (not to mention certain segments of the Church), is not sufficient to guarantee real power over public opinion. After fifteen years of Communist propaganda and control both of mass media and of youth organizations, Poland and Hungary have not been won over. The propaganda failed because it had to face both a fierce nationalism and enlightened and strong leadership, especially on the part of the Church. In other words, leadership, social cohesion, and a strong set of internalized values, can nullify even the most powerful efforts to mold minds.

Opinion Makers and Politics[5]

These points seem to be confirmed by certain American studies on the effects of political propaganda broadcast through the mass-media. Since these studies took place in normal circumstances where all parties had relative freedom to express their views, they are perhaps more help to us than totalitarian examples, when we come to assess opinion makers in our own societies. Moreover, their convergence with the observations made above suggests that we are probably dealing with basic and nearly universal factors.

The mass media have three principal effects on their audiences, though the incidence of these effects varies considerably. The first, and by far the most common, effect is the *preserving or confirmation effect*. This is to say that in most cases the mass media only reinforce the opinions people already have. They strengthen opinions more often than they change them. In other words the mass media are most effective when they are telling people, "you are right." The second or *activating effect* is far less common than the first, though far more common than the third or conversion effect. In activation the mass media make a person aware of his existing dispositions and show him how they can be formulated, and expressed in action. Here the media are catalysts rather than causes, organizers of latent opinion rather than creators. Such effects are, of course, most likely with individuals who have no formed opinion on a given subject.

Finally, there is the *conversion effect*, or the change from a previous opinion to a new one. This effect is relatively rare. Though there is not a great deal of evidence, it would appear that this effect is most common with those who are dissatisfied or troubled about their present opinion or are looking for a new one.

The same studies which concentrated on the effects of mass media in political campaigns, note, moreover, that the major influence on the opinions of the great majority is their group or groups. Friends, acquaintances and business associates are today, as in the past, the greatest formers of opinion. Experimental work indicates that face-to-face persuasion is still the most effective, and has not been replaced by the mass media.

Though the foregoing conclusions are stated without sufficient reservations and qualifications, they are sufficiently sound to enable us to draw certain other, important conclusions. Mass persuasion and opinion making on political topics become really dangerous only in the following cases. First, when the existing opinion which it reinforces is already unsound or poorly founded. Two, when there are large numbers of undecided voters whose basic dispositions are such that these voters can be activated in favor of dangerous views. Finally, when large numbers of people are in search of a new opinion for one reason or another. In brief, mass media persuasion and opinion making are most to be feared when the state of affairs is already bad, or where there is a vacuum to be filled. Of course, when the same opinion makers have also infiltrated local groups, that is, are using the oldest of techniques, the danger is heightened.

While opinion making by means of the mass media has very definite limits, at least as a force for changing the content of a people's opinion, organized opinion making has certain effects on the structure of communication that make it potentially very dangerous. Those who control the media, be they private interests or the state, can block the formation of organized opinions hostile to their interests and slow down the flow of useful information that they consider undesirable. Though this power is far from absolute, its very existence constitutes one of the unsolved problems of modern democratic societies. A word on each effect will help clarify the danger.

It is necessary to recall that ordinarily the opinion of individuals, even if widely held, cannot have full impact unless organized, and brought to bear on an issue. Thus, everyone in a given society may know that the government is corrupt and yet permit it to continue so without active protest. When the fact of corruption is brought into the public sphere and everyone discovers that everyone else is onto it too, it becomes possible to bring this opinion to bear in favor of reform. Usually this union of opinions can be obtained only by the use of the mass media, though there are numerous cases where it seems to occur spontaneously.

If reformers lack the funds to pay for mass media publicity, or if they are deliberately refused the use of such facilities, they can only with difficulty organize public opinion in the interests of change. As the high cost of mass communication leads to a greater and greater concentration of the media in the hands of a few, this blocking is liable to become more and more common.

Even when there is no direct and deliberate blocking of those who might seek to organize public opinion, there is a subtle sort of censorship which filters out information hostile to the interests of those who control the means of communication. As the media become more and more of a business proposition, and less and less of a real public service, their owners may tend to identify with the existing system, and see to it that hostile ideas are not circulated. Granted that the effects of such a situation are largely negative, they may still constitute a real danger. Indeed, as we shall see in the following sections on advertising and public relations, there are signs that the danger is increasing.

Advertising

We must at the start distinguish between the power of advertising to sell a product and its power to create a need or instill an idea. In the latter respect, advertising suffers from the same limitations as the mass media and political propaganda in general do. It can reinforce existing ideas, activate latent but unexpressed opinions, but only rarely can it cause a real change in opinion. Though advertising men often speak of creating needs and selling an idea of the good life, and though their critics accuse them of fostering materialism, advertising is more a reflection of the prevailing ideas than their cause. Even when advertising is actually the cause of some new idea or attitude, its success is probably due to favorable circumstances rather than to any great power inherent in advertising itself.

What, however, is to be said of advertising in relation to selling products? Studies conducted in the United States indicate that advertising is most effective when it supplies information that the consumer needs and wants. This may surprise many who think of advertising in terms of poetic persuasion, relying on all sorts of subtle techniques which appeal to our baser instincts; but in fact, advertising sells best when it tells the consumer what he can buy, where, and at what price.

The more persuasive types of advertising seem to be most effective when applied to a brand of some product which is already in use and which has emotional associations as well as a relatively low price. The persuasive advertisement works best in areas where people are not very rational in the first place, and where it seeks only to shift the choice from one brand to another. As one author has noted, it is fairly easy to shift consumers from beauty soap A to beauty soap B, but this does not mean that it is easy to teach people to use soap in the first place, or to change their whole attitude toward consumption, or toward life in general.

This last point has been demonstrated rather conclusively by Professor Borden in his work, *The Economic Effects of Advertising.*[6] When advertising is directed to the sale of a class of products rather than to the sale of a brand, its success is determined in great part by the fundamental tendencies at work in a society. If there is a tendency for people to buy automobiles, then advertising can push the sales up a bit; but if the tendency is in the opposite direction, as it was in the American recession of 1957-58, advertising is fairly helpless. It is interesting to note in this context that the trend to the small European car in the United States started with little or no advertising, and continued to advance despite the large sums spent advertising the big American cars. Similar examples could be presented involving cigars, beers, men's clothing, women's hats, and even certain soaps.

Advertising, moreover, cannot in general sell a bad product, though it may sell a mediocre one. The advertising men themselves insist on this point. You may sell the consumer a poor product once, but when he can test it for himself, no amount of advertising will get him to buy it again. The bigger advertising agencies are so conscious of this that they will not accept an inferior product lest they expose themselves to failure. This, of course, confirms an old principle of Dr. Goebbels, that propaganda is no good when the people can discover the truth for themselves.

Finally, though the general public hears only of successful advertising, many campaigns are real failures, and the vast majority are only mildly successful in increasing sales. In short, one is not dealing with magic that can overpower the public and send them scurrying to the store to buy the last product they saw advertised.

I have included these few remarks on the power of advertising to sell products because they reinforce what we already know about the power of the mass media and of propaganda in general. Despite all the talk of mysterious new techniques, advertising operates best where it is simply informing, or where it is reinforcing existing opinions and attitudes. Professional advertising men know this well, and I have seen reports of expensive campaigns being stopped when the company realized that they were swimming against the tide. I have seen other reports advising advertisers not even to begin, since the existing attitudes were too strong to be changed in less than twenty or thirty years. Here again, the real dangers come from the existing attitudes, or from a lack of attitudes coupled with a vague predisposition towards unsound opinions.

Despite all this, it must be confessed that the very existence of advertising on a large scale does pose certain problems for society. Because advertising supplies much of the financial support for the mass media, it has a certain impact on both the content and the structure of mass communication itself. Though the ultimate effects of these impacts are largely negative, they may be of some importance.

Because many media depend on advertising for their existence, and since their advertising revenues depend on their circulation, the media tend to provide what the public wants, rather than what it should have. Thus, to attract a mass audience, the content of magazines and newspapers is made very simple and attractive. The picture replaces the printed page, the pin-up replaces the serious political analysis, and the personality of political figures replaces any consideration of real issues and principles. The content of the mass circulation newspapers thus tends to be so diluted that the public is insulated from serious discussion of problems on the level of principle.

In the second place, the dependence of the media on advertising revenue makes them particularly vulnerable to pressures from the advertiser and the whole business community. Even in the absence of open coercion, the editor will hesitate to print an unpleasant story about a company that spends millions supporting his paper. It would be a rare human being who could resist all such temptations to temper his reporting to please his customers. There is, moreover, a certain amount of real coercion. How much I cannot say. Official investigations generally conclude that it is at a minimum, but the journalist himself will tell you many a story of the pressures that are brought to bear on him. Though it is impossible to give any precise estimate, the situation is a potential threat to the effective freedom of the press, and to the whole system of communication necessary to the functioning of a democracy.

Public Relations[7]

The profession of public relations counselor is so recent that many educated people have no clear idea of what it entails. Indeed, even those who practice public relations are in disagreement as to the function of their profession. Some people regard it as simply a means of getting free publicity; for others, it is a tool for counteracting opinions unfavorable to a company or institution; to others it is almost a way of life, or a philosophy, based on the premise that mutual understanding will bring about a new social order.

Despite this ambiguity, public relations are at the very least an effort to form the opinions of all those who have direct or indirect influence on the functioning of a given company, government bureau or other institution. The public relations man seeks to put his client's story before the public, to call attention to significant events affecting his company and even to modify the behavior of his company so that it will merit public approval.

Though it is hard to tell how successful public relations programs actually are, there are certain common practices in the profession which seem to pose real problems. Because so little is known about their effects, I shall only list them with a few words of comment.

First, many public relations experts attempt to penetrate the schools and, by winning the approval of the teachers, to introduce their literature into the curriculum itself. In some cases industry groups even attempt to influence the content, or else the use, of textbooks which might be hostile to their positions.

Such activities may pose a real threat to the independence of one of our most basic socializing forces.

Secondly, the news releases of the public relations experts, whether produced in the service of industry or government, are often printed by editors without any independent check on their truthfulness, bias or real purpose. Since public relations tends to be hidden propaganda, such a practice can lead to a breakdown of the reliability of the press.

Thirdly, though it is difficult to obtain evidence which can be used in the public forum, professionals admit that some bribery and pressure is used to place favorable stories in the media, and to tone down or suppress unfavorable news. If such practices continue to grow they may, in conjunction with advertising pressures, further weaken the communications structure.

Fourthly, the public relations expert often creates news events in order to attract public approval and attention. Though some of these events are mere stunts, others involve the creation of philanthropic foundations and institutes to serve some public need. Since the propaganda of fact is far more effective than the propaganda of words, such activities might constitute a real danger for a public which is unaware of their real significance.

Finally, since most public relations programs are long-range affairs, sometimes stretching over a period of twenty years, they may, by a process of erosion and gradual change, have effects which cannot be produced by short-term advertising and propaganda. This demands careful study; at present, we have no idea what the long-range effects of opinion making may be.

Even in the short run, however, the limited effects of public relations, advertising and propaganda, can be more important than the apparent facts indicate. Bills are passed and representatives elected on very small margins. Often, then, an opinion maker need only confirm one group in their opinions, and activate a small group of latent supporters, to attain the decisive effect. Moreover, because public relations men use not only mass media, but front organizations and organized grass roots movements, they can often penetrate small groups which do form opinion. Like it or not, those who can pay for such services can, in situations which are basically favorable to them, obtain significant results.

Some Conclusions and Implications

Though additional evidence may change the picture somewhat, two conclusions seem in order. First, the power of the opinion makers and the businesses which employ them is not unlimited. Secondly, in certain situations, business can exert a decisive influence over public opinion and all that depends on it.

This has important implications for the opinion makers, the schools, the churches and society, as well as for the business men who may hire professional communicators. The fact that opinion makers can be really successful in reinforcing attitudes which already exist, and in organizing latent opinion into consciously held positions, indicates that there is real danger only when unsound ideas and attitudes are already widely held, or when society is in such chaos that there is a vacuum of values and a longing for leadership. Even then, the would-be molders of minds can expect great success only if they are unopposed and if they control the small groups which are the dominant formers of opinion.

The vacuum and the state of social chaos may, of course, be brought about by wars, revolutions and natural catastrophes. However, they can also result from the failure of leadership and from the debility of the institutions charged with forming values and social attitudes, the church and the school in particular. There is evidence that the church and the school can lose much of their power when rapid economic and technological change have outstripped the understanding of teachers and clergymen. In such a situation they can no longer guide people effectively and society turns elsewhere for its ideas.

A second important implication lies not in the positive influence of opinion makers on public opinion, but in their negative influence on the structure through which much public information passes in a modern society. When the commercialization of the media has taken place, and the editor becomes a businessman rather than a publisher, he naturally tends to suppress opinion hostile to the economic status quo. Further, when he depends on advertising for his profits, he is subject to both direct and indirect pressures which may result in a suppression of information useful to the public. Finally, as the editor comes to accept biased sources of information—whether because of laziness, or self-interest—the very content of the media may become less and less trustworthy.

This combination of problems is far from simple. The danger does not arise merely from the malice of some unscrupulous individual, but from the economic and technological situation in which these professions operate. Society needs some form of mass communication, but this is expensive. Therefore, since the public is often unwilling to bear the expense directly, alternate means of support have grown up. In some nations the media are dominated by political parties, in others by the state, in yet others by private interests endowed with large resources. In any society the tendency is for those with money or power to control the mass media.

Further, we are not always clear as to what the media are, and what purpose they should serve. Intellectuals may assert that they should be vehicles of education and culture, but as matters stand, they are more often means of entertainment and escape. In theory, the media should serve only the public, in practice they must serve a variety of masters, including stockholders and advertisers.

Strangely enough, as we have said, even the opinion makers themselves are not always sure what they are. If we have referred to them as professionals, it was only in a very loose sense. Some see them as members of a new profession which has, or should take, its place beside the more traditional professions of teaching, preaching, law and medicine. Other opinion makers see themselves as mere technicians who have a skill to sell to the highest bidder. Others feel themselves to be only employees whose first allegiance is to their employers, and to stockholders. Though an effort has been made to clarify the social role of the opinion making professions there is as yet little significant agreement.

So long as the situation is ambiguous, the members of these professions often do not know what is expected of them and so tend to do what everyone else is doing. Since, moreover, they must often make decisions in which there are no clear and simple guides, and very little agreement about social goals, they must rely on a vague moral sense and on what they think is best. Indeed, it may be the lack of any useful norms that makes the new structure of communication such a potential danger to society. The problem of structures is a problem of values.

Even those opinion makers who have thought out their basic relationship to the public and have clear and solid ideas on their basic responsibility to protect the freedom of communication are often at a loss in particular cases. Dealing with a faceless mass, they do not know with any real certitude how their actions will affect others. Forced to make decisions on complicated issues, they often feel themselves incapable of judging what is correct or incorrect. On top of all this, the upright man is in competition with unscrupulous rivals, who will take over any dubious business that he passes up. Indeed, he is often in a position where too nice an insistence on principle may destroy his power to do any good in the long run.

The problem of structures and professional conduct is not

easy to solve. The professionals do not know what is expected of
them by society and are often without any norms. Even when
endowed with a real sense of responsibility, they can find themselves unable to judge concrete situations, and so are forced to
follow the accepted practices of their associates.

The groups of opinion makers, and the traditional opinion
forming institutions, have grave obligations in this area. The
schools and the church have not only a clear *ex officio* responsibility to form sound attitudes and ideas, but the tools as well.
Both these institutions have constant face-to-face contact with
men. Since these contacts are still the most effective in forming
opinions, they give to the church and schools potential power
and, consequently, responsibility. To blame everything on the
opinion makers is to dodge obligations and to excuse the ineffective use of the instruments available.

The opinion makers, journalists, writers, advertising men,
public relations practitioners and publicists, also have some definite obligations. Being in a position to influence public opinion
gives them a special responsibility for the effect of their acts.
They cannot excuse themselves on the ground that they are
hired hands, without abdicating all claim to being men and responsible citizens. It is not merely a question of avoiding such
obvious evils as slander, libel, the smear, the lie, and the un-
balanced presentation of the facts. It is also a matter of passing
judgment on the values they are to reinforce and on the causes
they serve. If they refuse to accept this challenge, they are
adopting the attitudes of those Nazi war criminals who pleaded
innocent, on the ground that they were only following orders.

The Responsibilities of Business

Firms that employ opinion makers have some power over public opinion, and are responsible accordingly. In the first place,

they certainly have an obligation to avoid all *direct* interference with the *editorial* content of the mass media. Attempts to suppress news of unemployment on the grounds that such news would hurt business, exemplify the types of interference which cannot help business and can certainly harm the public. Such tactics, though rare enough, are to be condemned except where business has reason to suspect that editors themselves are giving false information. Even then restraint is in order, since even a justified intervention may be very bad public relations.

Business certainly has a right and obligation to make sure that the *entertainment* it sponsors on radio and television is not offensive to public morals or good taste. This obligation arises not only from the necessity of avoiding any support of evil, but also from the need to protect the company against harmful associations. Despite the sometimes reasonable cries of those who resent commercial censoring of the arts, the influence of companies in this area has often been healthy. But the question is too complex to go into further here.

The real problem is generally not direct, but indirect, interference with editorial content. Thus, an editor who fears the loss of advertising may be tempted to tone down what he knows will be offensive to business. Some companies have, moreover, withdrawn advertising support of media because they disagreed with the editorial policy. The possibility of such boycott puts a tremendous power in the hands of certain large corporations and of the business community as a whole. What are their obligations here?

Obviously, business has *no obligation* to support media with which it disagrees. Indeed, if the media offend seriously against the public good, a firm may have an obligation to withdraw its advertising support. At the same time, because big business has an awesome potential power over media, there is certainly an obligation to act with restraint and only after a careful consideration of the facts. Business, like anyone who has power, is under an obligation to use it with care and respect for the good of others.

Unfortunately, the need for exercising such restraint and judgment obliges management to do what it may not be able to do: decide its own relation to the public good.

Even the limited power we have described makes business capable, in certain cases, of deciding which ideas shall rule and which laws shall be passed. In a way, business is expected to exercise a type of political authority and to act for the good of the entire nation. This implies that businessmen can successfully judge what is good for their own firms and good for the nation: a sort of enlightened despotism which, as one author has noted, is sure to end in revolution.[8]

Those thinkers who do not want to solve the problem call for the development of rebuttal power within the corporation. Because the large corporation is a type of political entity, they feel that it, like the state, must have a system of checks and balances. Dale, for example, suggests that the stockholders should be strengthened, free discussion encouraged, outside directors employed, and financial institutions encouraged to exercise their power.[9] While such means might mitigate the problem, they would not solve it. All the countervailing forces mentioned are still part of the business community as a whole. They might keep an individual corporation from overstepping just limits, but they would not guarantee the harmonizing of business interests with the good of the nation.

To be honest, we are faced with one of the great unsolved problems of modern social philosophy. Business has a duty to use its power responsibly, but it would appear that society needs means of insuring that this be done. Perhaps we need carefully written constitutions for corporations. Perhaps we need a form of corporate federalism.[10] Certainly we need a great deal of study by businessmen, scholars and political figures.

The necessity of this study would seem to impose one important limit on the use of business's opinion making power. At present much of this power is used to reinforce the old idea that competition takes care of the problem, or to promote the impression that a socially responsible business community can be trusted with the power. Often, those who dare to raise the question are branded enemies of business, socialists, or communist sympathizers. This has kept the public seriously retarded and has stifled thoughtful discussion of the question.

It is suggested, then, that business has some obligation to halt the obstruction of discussion, to broaden its own perspective, and to face the awful possibility that it might have more power than is good for either the nation or the business community.

Notes

1. Some of the material in this chapter is taken from my article "Les Fabricants d'Opinion," *Information Catholiques Internationales*, 1 December 1960, no. 133, pp. 15-26. For additional material and a bibliography of social psychology *cf.* my book *An Introduction to Some Ethical Problems of Modern American Advertising* (Rome: Gregorian University Press, 1961).

2. *Cf.* Adolf A. Berle, Jr., *Power Without Property* (Harcourt, Brace, 1959), pp. 110-116.

3. Most of my information in this section is drawn from an unpublished lecture by Dr. Mayer, who was in charge of the psychological investigation of the veterans returning from the Korean war.

4. *Cf.* Hadley Cantril, *The Psychology of Social Movements* (John Wiley and Sons, 1941).

5. Probably the best studies on this topic are: Paul Lazarsfeld *et al.*, *The People's Choice* (Columbia University Press, 1944) and Bernard R. Berelson *et al.*, *Voting: A Study of Opinion Formation in a Presidential Campaign* (University of Chicago Press, 1954).

6. (Irwin, 1942).

7. *Cf.* Stanley Kelley, *Professional Public Relations and Political*

Power (Johns Hopkins, 1956). J.A.R. Pimlott, *Public Relations and American Democracy* (Princeton University Press, 1951).

8. Peter F. Drucker, *The New Society* (Harper and Brothers, 1949), p. 281.

9. Ernest Dale, "Management Must Be Made Accountable," *Harvard Business Review*, March-April, 1960 (vol. 38, no. 2), pp. 49-59; and "The Social and Moral Responsibilities of the Executive in the Large Corporation," *American Economic Review*, May, 1961 (vol. 51, no. 2), pp. 540-548.

10. *Cf.* Edward S. Mason (ed.), *The Corporation in Modern Society* (Harvard University Press, 1959), chapters 1, 4, 5 and 11.

10 BUSINESS AND WASTE

LIKE SO MANY PUBLIC DEBATES, the dispute about business and waste has been carried on in rather emotional terms. Writers like Mr. Vance Packard, the author of those best sellers, *The Hidden Persuaders, The Status Seekers* and *The Waste Makers*,[1] take a dim view of the situation. While his attacks on planned and psychological obsolescence have a convincing ring, they tell only one side of the story. Pierre Martineau, a prominent figure in advertising, counters by saying that obsolescence actually contributes to the quality of products.[2] Others claim that the waste is merely superficial since it is a necessary factor in an economy whose growth depends on increases in consumption. A third group sees no problem at all. Samuel Y. Hyde supported this view when he wrote in *America*:

The thesis of this study is that advertising is not immoral, per se, and that it operates within the bounds of Christian Ethics in seeking to persuade consumers to buy goods and services, *whether or not such goods and services are needed*.[3] (Italics added)

Despite such disagreements, surveys by *Printers' Ink* and *The Harvard Business Review* reveal that the thoughtful business-man is concerned by waste in the form of planned obso-lescence.[4] Unfortunately, not everyone is talking about exactly the same thing. For some, planned obsolescence is synonymous with the frequent introduction of superficial product changes, styling, and prestige selling. Others take it to mean a policy of holding back new product improvements until sales for the existing models decline. Yet a third group uses the term to designate built-in obsolescence, that is, a way of manufacturing products so that they will wear out rapidly. Though this latter policy poses some ethical problems, the present chapter uses the definition adopted by *Printers' Ink*:

Planned obsolescence is here defined as yearly or other regular superficial changes in products, styling or prestige selling appeals to persuade the public to purchase new items before the old are worn out.[5]

A definition is of some help, but it leaves the great questions unanswered. How much planned obsolescence is there in the American economy? What is its significance for business, the consumer and the nation? When does it involve real waste and so become an ethical problem?

The extent of planned obsolescence has not been determined by any scientific means. Moreover, businessmen themselves vary widely in their estimates of both its extent and its significance.[6] There is good reason for this. How are we to tell when a change is merely superficial? How do we know that the consumer buys the new product because of the superficial change and not for some more rational reason? Even if styling, or prestige, are prime motives, does buying the new product really amount to waste?

Though it is currently popular to answer all these questions in a way unfavorable to business, the real answers are not easy to come by. Even the few facts about advertising given in the previous chapter indicate that buying is influenced by very basic forces. Business may encourage these, but ordinarily it does not create them. Granted that style, newness and prestige, may be marginal buying motives, the consumer is generally buying a whole package of goods, most of whose contents have real utility.

The automotive and appliance industries are often accused of encouraging waste by their annual model changes. However, there are facts to indicate that the waste may be much less than is popularly believed.[7] In the first place, the new model generally has new and real mechanical improvements mixed in the package with styling. Power brakes, power steering, the torsion bar suspension and added safety factors, generally accompany such things as fins and chrome. Secondly, those who can finance a new model often find that they save money in the long run because repairs have become so expensive. Finally, the used car and used appliance market absorbs the older models so that the physical resources are intact.

Certainly, there appears to be waste in the retooling that accompanies model changes, but it is difficult to say how much of it is the price of real improvements and selling points and how much is true waste. We do not know the answers to these questions. Only the businessmen involved can decide the question of fact. Consequently, the present chapter is not an attack on waste in business, but an attempt to develop the principles which should guide the businessman once he has the facts.

The Moral Problem

Though about two thirds of the businessmen polled see some sort of a problem in planned obsolescence, there is little agreement as to what the problem actually is. Some see the waste as part of the inculcation of materialism; for others it is bad because we still need schools and hospitals; a third group condemns it as a criminal waste of non-reproducible natural re-

sources. For some few, it is a question of loss of international
prestige or of falling behind in the race with Russia.

What is perhaps more interesting is the variety and quality of
the arguments used in favor of planned obsolescence. As many
as 50% agree that a large proportion of sales based on styling
changes and prestige buying is the inevitable result of a high
standard of living. A smaller group feels that if we were forced
to drop product obsolescence, the economy would not stand the
resulting drop in sales. Oddly enough, 30% of those who saw a
problem did not feel that it was the responsibility of business to
decide if the consumer needs schools more than he needs tail-
fins.[8]

Thus, the moral problem has several dimensions. Here, only
three will be treated: the problem of materialism, the problem
of individual need, and the problem of social need in the United
States. Though the international dimension is of extreme importance, it would call for a longer book.

Materialism

Business is accused of encouraging and preaching materialism
by means of its advertised vision of the good life. As the critics
see it, this is not merely a question of selling goods, but of
attempting to convince the public that the good life consists
exclusively, or nearly so, in the possession and use of gadgets,
gimmicks and the accouterments of modern living. According to
the more articulate critics, advertising, the tool of business,
preaches a gospel pretty close to pure hedonism. The critics
often have some interesting ammunition, because some advisors
to business have advocated deliberate attempts to implant a
materialistic hedonist philosophy in the public mind.

The ethician, unlike the popular writer, cannot be satisfied
with such vague charges. He wants to draw the line between

legitimate use of material goods, and uses which are harmful to the total growth of the person. Further, he wants to know whether the meanings the critic finds in advertising are really there, or whether there have been unconscious misinterpretations.

Any effort to draw the line between legitimate and illegitimate uses of material goods must first meet the problem of the old-time puritanism. Puritanism tended to be hostile to all comfort, on the grounds that it distracted men from the important things in life. Thrift, the simple life, such mottoes as "Do, make do, do without" were part of the stuff of practical puritanism. In time of need and scarcity there was much to recommend practical rules of this sort. Unfortunately, the rules were made absolute in many minds, and pleasure, comfort, expenditure became suspect in and of themselves.

Puritanism is vanishing, but its traces still distort thinking and give rise to rash, rhetorical, and unfounded ethical judgments. Sound ethics recognizes that material goods and services are meant to satisfy legitimate human needs and desires. If the growth of the individual is helped along by the satisfaction of such needs and desires, the goods and services are basically ethical. It may be difficult to allocate properly, but this should not blind us to the fact that the material side of things has more value than the puritans allowed.

Leaving aside the rules which should govern the relative allocation of resources, let us take a look at the range of needs which can legitimately be satisfied by the economic order. These considerations will help us not only to clarify our thought about materialism, but to decide what constitutes waste. So long as a material good or service satisfies a real human need and contributes to the growth of the whole man, there can be no question of *absolute* waste. If, in addition, needs are satisfied in the right order, with the proper balance between the public and the private spheres, there will not even be *relative* waste.

Human Needs

Human needs are extensive and varied both in their nature and in the urgency for their satisfaction. They extend from the biological level to the social, and on to the psychological, esthetic, moral and religious. Though people tend to think of material goods and services as satisfying only biological needs, the material world also serves the social and psychological development of man.

Man, being composed of both body and spirit, obviously needs things for the support of the body: food, clothing, housing, medical care, etc., but he also needs certain psychic satisfactions: entertainment, recreation, education. Here, a whole range of material things can be used with great profit. Though it is often forgotten by the puritan school of thought, man also needs leisure and freedom from drudgery so that he can satisfy his need for beauty, fantasy, and most of all for prayer and contemplation. Material things which free him for these purposes can be real goods in an ethical sense. Finally, man has social needs for communication and union with his fellow man. The mass media, modern transport, social gatherings, all contribute to the satisfaction of these needs. Here, too, there is place for material things such as clothing and housing which, in addition to fulfilling basic requirements, also symbolize a man's position in society.

Many of the classic writers summed this up by saying that man could legitimately use all those things necessary for sustaining life, for living it decently and comfortably, and for expressing one's position in society. None of these points is fixed, however, and as both man and society develop, the possibilities of self-development are enlarged, so that it becomes possible to use a large number of things in a reasonable way. Indeed, there is a dynamic and reciprocal relation between needs and the possibility of satisfying them, so that the mutual development of these increases the possibility of both economic and true cultural growth.

Quite obviously material things can dominate a man, destroy his balance, and shorten his perspectives. The danger, however, comes from within the individual, rather than from the material world of today. Indeed, the real danger arises when our cultural and spiritual growth does not keep pace with that technological advance which opens up such tremendous vistas to the individual who is ready for them.

Almost intuitively, man sees that there is a hierarchy contained in these needs, which imposes a certain direction and measure on all use of material goods and services. The man who roots himself on the lower part of the scale becomes an animal, a selfish, egotistical being, almost a caricature of human nature. The temptation to disregard the upper level is always present, but our own good demands that we subordinate the lower to the higher, or better, that we coordinate all values.

Though the lower values must always be ordered to the higher ones and ultimately to the final perfection of man, the *temporal order* in which these are to be realized depends not only on the dignity of a given value but on the urgency and necessity for its realization at a given moment. Man, being conditioned by the limitations of time and space, cannot satisfy all needs simultaneously. While the satisfaction of some needs can be postponed without serious consequence, others must be tended to at once if man is to continue in existence: thus basic needs for food, clothing and housing, cannot be postponed without serious harm to the organism.

In the temporal order the absolutely necessary takes precedence over the merely useful, and the useful over the pleasant. Often, indeed, the immediately urgent must be cared for as a preparation for the attainment of the higher values. But we must remember that the postponement of the attainment of higher values is ethical only so long as the higher values are not destroyed in the process. Thus, a man who continues to amass money so that he may leave his children wealthy, fails, if he has become a miser or a tyrant in the process. So too, a man cannot sacrifice his religious faith, his sanity, or the health of his family merely to prolong his own life, for this would be the frustration of his own dignity.

The temporal element also obliges man to consider the future when making choices. A future need may oblige one to forego some present satisfaction, even a useful and lawful one. Thus there is an obligation to prepare for sickness, old age and all reasonable expectations of future needs. Man is not free to let tomorrow take care of itself, when some effort today can provide against the ordinary contingencies.

Some Conclusions and Comments

In view of what has been said, it is easy to see that business can legitimately supply an almost infinite number of goods to satisfy real human needs. Even style changes and prestige can have meaning if the one satisfies a need for beauty and the other a reasonable need for manifesting achievement. This is to say that goods used for such purposes cannot be said to be wasted in any *absolute* sense.

The real problem, however, is centered on relative rather than absolute waste. Thus, if planned obsolescence makes it difficult to satisfy higher and more urgent needs, because resources have been diverted to the fulfilling of lesser needs, desires or whims, it has caused waste, or at least encouraged it. The T.V. aerial over the tarpaper shack and the Cadillac delivering children to the substandard school are signs of relative waste.

While business may have an obligation to avoid promoting such waste, the consumer also has duties. Unless the buyer has a proper sense of values, business efforts to fulfill moral responsibilities can often be futile. Moreover, because the roots of the problem are found in the ethos—that is the value atmosphere of a nation—the school, the church and civic organizations must also face the possibility that they have been remiss.

In addition, certain institutional aspects of American life need reform. You can buy a television set with a small down payment, but it requires a great deal of saving to buy a house. As a result, people will often buy what they can get, rather than what they need. To remedy such situations, society requires further redistribution of income, new credit institutions, and more economical forms of health insurance, as well as a reorientation of values. The business community certainly has some obligation to promote such changes, but we must face the fact that government intervention may be necessary: particularly since the most crucial problem is in the area of social consumption.

The Social Dimension

The economy exists to satisfy the needs of all men, and not merely the needs of those who have purchasing power. Not all the needs of men, moreover, can be satisfied by the market economy. As a result both private, nonprofit groups and the state are needed to redistribute income and to satisfy certain human needs. Private schools, hospitals, charitable organizations, and cultural groups, all operate to supply goods, often material, which are not adequately handled by the business community. The government supplements these efforts with such things as the public schools, the defense establishment, tax exemptions for nonprofit groups, social insurance, relief assistance and public works.

This is as it should be. We may grumble about taxes, but we all recognize that they are, on the whole, necessary if society is to function properly. We complain about certain provisions of the "welfare state," but are forced to admit that many of these do fulfill real social needs. Unfortunately, even in the midst of our complaining, there is a temptation to think that, having put up with taxes and state intervention, we have fulfilled our obligations to our fellow man.

In our more candid moments, however, we recognize that there are other obligations. It is unlawful to destroy our own property on a whim, since this harms others. It is unethical to indulge in waste, not only because it is unreasonable, but because there are others in need. In addition, all but the most hardhearted admit that there is some obligation to help others directly, even when it means a sacrifice of legitimate satisfactions, or a lowering of one's own standards of living. All this is not only sound ethics, but embedded in our laws and in our society as a whole.

There are, moreover, very special obligations which arise when, having satisfied our own needs, and established a reasonable standard of living, we are left with a surplus. An individualist of the egotistical brand might say that it is his money and he is free to do what he likes with it. Actually, however, there remains an obligation to see that such a surplus is put to the best possible use. Wealth, after all, has meaning only insofar as it is used to attain valid human goals.

When applying his surplus to the satisfaction of the needs of others, a man may choose between investment, charity and philanthropy. By investing in industries which supply both work and useful articles, he creates conditions which enable others to help themselves. Sometimes, the surplus can be applied directly to the alleviation of suffering or to the creation of private institutions which will serve the public weal. All three methods are consistent with the right goal of wealth and the choice depends on what is the best possible use, here and now, in a given economy and culture.

American students of the question, Galbraith being among the most prominent,[9] believe that business diverts necessary resources from this semi-public and public sector to the production of goods which, while satisfying some need, are not of first importance. The critics feel that as a result of this diversion of resources, education, health, public culture, and basic research, have been neglected. The result is a waste, albeit relative, of our wealth.

Business is blamed for much of this mal-allocation, because its advertising stresses private consumption and its propaganda fights government intervention even in necessary fields. Granted that business may be guilty of reinforcing attitudes which lead to this situation, we must recognize that other forces are at work. In other words, we are once again faced with an ethical problem which is common to both business and the larger society.

If education is underdeveloped, it is because politicians and the public are reluctant to vote increased funds for education, or to pay adequate salaries: consumption of goods comes first. But business is not the only cause of this narrow attitude. Further, there is considerable waste on the part of educators. Often funds go for mammoth stadia, for cosmetology laboratories—even in general high schools—and for all sorts of auxiliary services of a noninstructional nature. Indeed, there can be serious doubts about the productivity of American education itself.

A similar situation exists in the field of health. Money is in short supply here too, partly because doctors, hospitals, etc. have often lagged in the search for more effective methods of finance and cost control. One wonders if the medical profession is not as guilty as any other group.

Obligations

As noted at the start of this chapter, there is room for research on the scale and impact of planned obsolescence. Until the results of such study are available, business cannot be found guilty of all the crimes it is accused of. Even so, it is possible to assign several broad responsibilities to the business community.

If model changes and prestige selling, aided by advertising, actually reinforce and activate a tendency to divert resources from necessary public services, business will have some obligation to moderate its present policies. Two points, however, should be kept in mind. First, a withdrawal from advertising and from planned obsolescence would not solve the problem, which is the result of other and probably more powerful social forces. Secondly, such a withdrawal would have to be gradual lest it cause economic dislocation. All this, of course, is hypothetical, based on the assumption that business policies of obsolescence do have some significant effect on the distribution of resources.

In line with what was said in the previous chapter, business may have a far more serious obligation with regard to its propaganda and lobbying. Since such activities can be decisive in influencing marginal votes in the legislature, business may be able to block the passage of laws which are necessary for the fulfillment of social needs. Consequently, there is an obligation to go beyond traditional considerations of what is good for business, and to consider the real needs of the nation.

In particular, business would do well to examine some of the unfounded arguments which it has used to justify its policies. As I have tried to show in chapters 6 and 7, some of these merely serve to obscure real issues, to arouse critics, and to divert business from its own technical shortcomings.[10] Business, for example, might do well to ask if some needs are unfulfilled because management has not been willing to enter new fields.

In a speech to the American Marketing Association, J. B. McKitterick of General Electric has this to say:[11]

By hindsight, then, the capacity that stands idle in the manufacturing sector might have been invested in the service sector with highly profitable effects not only on business, but on the growth of the economy as a whole. . . .

By degrees, it therefore becomes clear that the penalty for investing with an overly narrow concern for competitive survival in a given market and too little regard for the needs of the whole society, is not merely a loss of profit for the business due to excess capacity and falling prices, but a loss of economic growth due to increasing diversion of the consumer's purchasing power to the least efficient sectors that contribute to his total cost of living.

Even if business does not assume these responsibilities, the alternative is not necessarily government intervention. Many of the problems can be solved by the strengthening, or the creation, of private organizations which serve social needs. This may involve government subvention, if there is no other way, but at present there is still an alternative. If business is really interested in controlling big government, it should increase its aid to those groups which are struggling to satisfy needs which are not cared for by the market economy.

It must be recognized that the elimination of both absolute and relative waste depends not only on business but on the public it serves. Even if one admits that business can influence public tastes, individuals can still direct the economy by enlightened choices in the market and by unselfish acceptance of sound social legislation.

At the same time, business should recall that the vast scope of human needs gives it room for creative work which has real human meaning and ethical significance. What it must do is to search for the real needs, and to stop what are often futile efforts to exploit mere desire. What is needed is imagination, not only in the production and distribution of goods, but in the creation of new financial institutions. In short, business must accept the real challenge rather than cling to the narrow, conservative philosophy of the outworn classical business creed.

Notes

1. (David McKay, 1957, 1959, 1960).
2. "Martineau Says Obsolescence Results in Quality," *Advertising Age*, July 31, 1961, p. 3.
3. "Is Advertising Moral?", *America*, March 11, 1961, p. 760.
4. "Planned Obsolescence," *Printers' Ink*, May 19, 1961, pp. 23-29; May 26, 1961, pp. 23-31. John B. Stewart, "Problems in Review: Planned Obsolescence," *Harvard Business Review*, September-October, 1959, pp. 14-28; 168-176.
5. *Printers' Ink*, May 19, 1961, p. 23.
6. *Ibid.*, p. 25.
7. *An Introduction to Some Ethical Problems of Modern American Advertising* (Rome: Gregorian University Press, 1961), esp. pp. 167-170.
8. Stewart, *op. cit.*, p. 24.
9. John K. Galbraith, *The Affluent Society* Boston: Houghton Mifflin, 1958).
10. *Cf.* note 7. Chapters six and seven of this work give a critical and technical analysis of the argument that advertising is necessary to stimulate consumption as a means of insuring economic growth.
11. Reprinted in *Advertising Age*, July 23, 1962, p. 75.

11 PROFESSIONS, ASSOCIATIONS AND CODES

No ONE CAN STUDY business ethics even casually without considering the professional associations and professional codes of conduct. Even though there is a great deal of cynicism about these topics, they are worthy of serious and balanced consideration. In the first place the professionalization of business and the formulation of codes appear to be necessary, though not infallible, means of improving business practices. In the second place, the various business associations are probably the best, if not the only, institutions capable of fostering such improvement.

Is Business a Profession?

Many modern executives, because they are hired managers and not owners, see themselves as members of an inchoate profession with its own rules and responsibilities.[1] Though the number of such managers seems to be growing, there is yet doubt as to whether business as a whole is, or can be, a suitable ground for the development of a profession in the ordinary sense of the word. Large groups of managers, indeed, do not want to accept professionalism, or the responsibilities that go with it.[2] Despite the disagreement, it seems necessary to discover what sort of professionalism might be possible and useful in the market place.

Bunting lists eight requirements for the establishment of a profession:[3]

1. Establishment of the field to be covered.
2. Provision of an ethical code.
3. Provision of rules for membership.
4. Development of educational standards.
5. Provision for an administrative code.
6. Establishment of penalties for noncompliance.
7. Establishment of an education degree.
8. Provision of the service motive.

Even at first glance it is obvious that business has not, and probably cannot, fulfill all these conditions. However, while business may not aspire to be a profession in a strict sense, it can possibly move towards the ideal. Indeed, if we break the question down it becomes clear that some segments of the business community are professions, and that business itself contains many employees who are professionals. The public accountant realizes all the provisions given above, and the consulting managerial engineer satisfies many of them. Doctors, lawyers, psychologists and research men are professionals before they are businessmen. Some others, such as public relations consultants (as distinct from mere practitioners) are also moving in the direction of professional standards. In addition, though the small proprietor may have no concern but profit, the class of hired managers, especially in the larger corporations, are becoming conscious that their behavior is governed not so much by self-interest as by the good of the organization, the interests of society, and the prescriptions of law.

Many businessmen recognize that business in general, as well as their own firms and the public, is threatened by the presence of inexperienced or unprincipled—elements in business. As one man put it, the rhetorician or fast talker is the curse of business.

He talks himself into a job he cannot handle, and before you catch up with him, he has done all sorts of harm in attempting to cover up his incompetence. There is a feeling, then, that all elements affected by business would benefit from some sort of "professional" control.

There are, of course, less noble and more mundane motives advanced. Some want status and feel that professionalization will help to promote it: thus (perhaps) confusing ends and means. Others, fearful of increased government intervention, see professionalization, private licensing, and private enforcement, not only as a means of increasing status and business ethics but of keeping the government out of business.

The arguments against professionalization are sometimes even less noble. Often the critics feel that they, in their particular business, cannot afford to operate on a high professional plane. This is often linked with the old idea that ethics is a luxury.

Although this next idea seldom finds its way into print, interviews indicate that many are biased against the professional approach because they feel that they would never have been allowed in, during the good old days. This attitude is often found in the self-made man who has clawed his way up from the bottom. It is understandable, emotionally powerful, but not too cogent.

At the same time, there are some important arguments against the professionalization of business. A profession involves a restriction of membership. Though this already exists, especially in regard to top management in major corporations, it is doubtful whether such restrictions would not do more harm than good if applied to business as a whole. An open market demands free entry, and so does the fostering of individual initiative and entrepreneurial endeavor.

The problem seems to focus on the difficulty of establishing standards for admission to business, and even to the higher ranks of management. Both business in general and particular businesses depend on members who possess human qualities as well as knowledge. These qualities, despite psychological testing, are not capable of accurate, much less of standardized objective measurement. As a result, it would be difficult to set up selective criteria for many jobs. Nevertheless, licensing is required for insurance salesmen, for the customers' representatives of stock brokers, as well as for accountants, real estate agents, and architects: so it should be possible to set up minimum intellectual standards for many other kinds of business.

Though there are obstacles to even a partial professionalization of many sectors of business, they are not always insurmountable. And though there is a price to pay, the rewards could be great. Professionalism, with its stress on service and group membership for the welfare of society, could help to alleviate some of the tensions which were considered in the chapters on responsibility and work. In other words, such a change might restore meaning to an area of life which for the past few centuries has been considered as a classic locus of selfishness.

Associations and the Professional Outlook

Even a partial "professionalization" of business, and of particular groups within the business community, cannot be realized without strong associations and vigorous leadership. This is trite, but it deserves emphasis, since there is sometimes a naive expectation that the millennium will come by itself. Granted that outside forces, both personal and impersonal, may stimulate professional growth, the real causes must be inside the business world.

Unfortunately, many trade associations are no more than lobbies or clearing houses for information. Both functions are legitimate and necessary, but they tend to narrow the preoccupation of the groups involved. Associations will often push for legislation which is favorable to themselves but which ignores the public. To put it another way, the associations are tools of defense and not instruments for fulfilling the social obligations of the group.[4]

This narrow focus is understandable since the trade associations often came into existence as defensive instruments and at a time when social responsibility was not in the air. Today, however, when there is an increasing realization that the good of business depends on its reputation and on its ability to serve the broader community, associations should have some concern with the formation of their members and with increased service to the public. Even if this were not demanded by general ethical principles, self-love and a broad concept of self-defense should urge the associations toward it.

Much more than self-interest is involved in this question. The public is increasing its demand for regulation of business because private groups, such as trade associations, have not shown themselves capable of discharging collective, that is industry, responsibility. In the absence of an effective private means of discharging collective responsibilities, the sphere of government intervention will increase. This may not harm business, though it probably will, but it is a dangerous erosion of the sphere of private and individual liberty.

The real nature of this threat to liberty appears when one studies the manner in which the government itself has gone about regulation. Because the ordinary judicial channels are already overloaded, the government has established regulatory agencies which are law making bodies, as well as being executive and judicial agencies. Here many of the traditional checks and balances are absent. Here, too, there is frequently too little protection of the right of due process, as well as a vagueness in both law and interpretation.[5] Granted the climate of public opinion, however, there is no alternative to such bodies except effective organization of private business associations.

At present, some associations have arrived at this concept,

others are struggling toward it, but many still act as if they were living in the nineteenth century. Interviews with businessmen indicate several interesting reasons for this. The most common seems to be a lack of vigorous leadership. This is not an accident, but a result of the way associations are set up. The real work of associations is generally done by a class of professional administrators who are hired employees of the group. They are not directly involved in business, and often have not been businessmen. As a result, they cannot be expected to give leadership, because they lack both the prestige and the independence to do so. Even sincere executives in such groups are liable to remember that they can be ousted by those who pay the bills.

The people capable of giving real leadership, the businessmen themselves, often do not have the time for, or the interest in, the affairs of the association. Furthermore, if they did attempt to get too far ahead of the pack, they would run the risk of being labelled reformers or do-gooders. Even the leader has to keep his eye on the movement of the society he belongs to.

One successful business leader in association work informed me that his real task was the education of the members who had decision making power. As he saw it, it would take twenty years to make them (1) understand what was at issue and (2) form an ethical consensus favorable to real progress in his field. This seems to be realistic. Indeed, the prime obligation today would seem to be an effort to educate on this level and to move towards the creation of a broader sense not only of social responsibility, but of identification with the business group.

Though no one can expect a complete reform to result from such educational activities, there is evidence that the atmosphere of a firm or an industry, and the example of superiors, are powerful factors in ethical conduct. Human nature being what it is, there is a built-in tendency to do what is expected of us: not an infallible tendency, but enough to be a potential force in raising standards.

In view of their task, the associations need better leadership.

Retired businessmen, drawn from the particular field to be organized and improved, would probably be most effective. In addition to having the prestige which comes with success, they would be endowed with time and a long-range perspective. Elder statesmen such as Clarence Randall and J. C. Penney have already done much in this direction. What is needed now is an extension of the idea and of the practice.

Leaders are ineffective unless there are active followers. People who feel that something should be done, must recognize their obligation to join associations and to participate in their affairs. Too often the really talented man allows himself to become trapped into running minor affairs in his church or community and so neglects those areas of business where he could make a truly significant contribution to society. Obviously, the temptation is to let George do it, but this will not guarantee that the job will be done, let alone done correctly.

There are two additional obstacles to a growth of effective associations. The first is a fear of anti-trust actions; the second, a hesitancy about acting as a conscience for one's brother.

Though outsiders may consider the fear of anti-trust prosecution to be exaggerated, it is real and grounded. In the past, associations have been prevented from enforcing standards, and the law is such that it may occur again.[7] Even if the attorney general should give the group an assurance that he would not prosecute, individuals who felt they had been harmed could bring a civil suit and, if successful, claim damages. Realistically, then, there is need for some revision of the anti-trust laws, if there are to be any sort of effective associations. Such reform will not be easy, for at times the associations have acted in a restraint of trade.[8] Any revision of the law will involve a careful calculation of the public good, case by case.

The reluctance to act as one's brother's keeper is rather strongly rooted in the American character. If business is to overcome it, the idea must be disseminated that, like it or not, business can be hurt by the erring, weak and crooked. An increasing sense of the interdependence of businessmen must be developed. Obviously, this will also demand a corresponding growth of social conscience on the part of American society as a whole. Business, after all, cannot rise too far above the general moral ethos of the society in which it operates. This may not be an excuse, but it is a fact of life.

It may be difficult to develop a sense of real community among businessmen, but it is not impossible. While doing research in England and Holland, the present author was struck by how certain groups had such a highly developed sense of mutual interest that mere social pressure was enough to curtail many unethical practices. Membership in some associations was like membership in an exclusive club. Members were expected to fulfill certain duties or be expelled, if not from business, at least from association with their peers.[9]

Codes

Though an increasing number of groups have attempted to draw up, and even enforce, codes of business practice, there is still a great deal of cynicism about them, even when there is no vocal opposition.[10] As so often happens, the cynicism results not merely from experience with existing codes, but from the idea that codes are supposed to solve all problems in theory and practice. Because of idealism on the one hand, and deliberate obstructionism on the other, many codes are meaningless bits of propaganda rather than real guides for action. Several executives in one trade association did not know they had an ethical code, though it had been revised in the previous year. Some businesses attempt to keep their codes vague, even in areas capable of precise definition, lest they offend anybody in the business. Many, of course, will sign codes as long as the codes have no teeth, but will fight sanctions as if they were the tool of the devil.

For all this, properly drawn up codes can have a useful if limited function. First, and perhaps most important, they can have a real educational effect. Secondly, they can narrow the area in which a man has to struggle with doubts. Thirdly, they can be a visible, impersonal standard which men of good will can use to support their decisions.

The educational utility of codes must be seen against the hurly burly of everyday business life. The businessman, especially in his earlier years, may have neither the time nor the experience to figure out what is right and wrong in his field. A code, if fairly detailed, supplies him with certain guide lines based on the experience and thought of others. If nothing else, it makes him aware that there are moral problems peculiar to his business, which cannot be resolved in a vacuum or by some vague feeling in the pit of his stomach.

By giving some guide lines, codes also help to cut into the area of doubt. Granted that they cannot cover every possible situation, they can still enable a man to handle the ordinary problems with ease. That they can do no more, only proves that they suffer from the weakness of all human formulations.

Many codes cannot fulfill even these limited functions. Often, they are no more than a form of industry etiquette and avoid all real moral problems.[11] Others are short, vague and pious creeds which do little but say that the group is against sin and for democracy and free enterprise. Yet others, while making an attempt at some detail, omit really specific mention of many obligations to clients and the public. It is little wonder, then, that the codes are ineffective and inspire such remarks as the following:

When businessmen talk ethics, it is time for the public to be suspicious. "Business Ethics" usually means a conspiracy against the public to keep in existence high-cost producers and give more than handsome protection to the efficient low-cost firms.[12]

If codes are to be in any way effective, they must be definite and include all major areas of ethical concern. This is not merely a question of common sense, but has been established by research.[13] Unless a code contains clear definitions of situations, it cannot have educational effect. A detailed code like that of the National Association of Broadcasters is to be preferred to the vague general statements contained in the Principles for Business Conduct adopted by the Chamber of Commerce of the United States.[14]

A realistic code must be concerned with more than the good of the company and its officers. It must relate to the prescriptions of law, the interests of society and of all the groups with which a corporation deals.[15] It should attempt to give a fairly complete picture of the ethical dimensions of the businessman's role.[16] In drawing up such a code, an association might use the questions and headings proposed by the Business Ethics Advisory Council.[17] While the statement of the Council is far from complete, it does indicate some of the more important points to be considered. The American Management Association's collection of both association and company codes, though still only in its infancy, offers another starting point for those who recognize the need for careful work in this area.[18]

The adoption of a code, no matter how complete and detailed, is not enough. New members of a firm or association need to study the code, see the reasons for its provisions, and understand its general importance as a part of business life. This means systematic indoctrination by upper management or its representatives. While even this may not be enough, it is a necessary minimum.

Sanctions

If a code is to be more than a canonization of existing practices, it must have sanctions. Businessmen will admit that the lack of penalties is the most basic reason why even well constructed codes have not had a significant impact in many industries. Business, of course, faces real problems in working out sanctions. First, it must fear anti-trust prosecution when it operates through an association. Second, unlike such professions as medicine, law and accounting, it does not have the full support of public authority.[19] Despite these difficulties, there are several things which can be done to make regulations more than a public relations tool.

In the first place individual firms have the power to discipline employees who violate the code. Discipline of this sort requires integrity and courage, but, as Peter Drucker has noted, integrity is an essential management virtue.[20] Unless management is ready to stand by its avowed principles and to enforce them, no progress can be made either in ethics or in business itself.

The associations, moreover, are not completely powerless. They can publicize industry codes and violations in such a way as to win public support and exert a real social control over offenders. Publicity given by Dun and Bradstreet in its credit ratings is said to have much to do with raising ethical standards in the credit field. There is some reason to think that exposure might stimulate progress in other sectors.

Understandably, associations do not want to wash their dirty linen in public. However, if this is the only, or the best, way to obtain compliance, in the present order of things it may be necessary. Certainly, the Bulletins of the Better Business Bureau, which already attempt to publicize abuses of one type, do not seem to have hurt business. On the contrary, they have increased public confidence in the ethics of many retailers.

The successful administration of a program of this sort will demand strong and stable leadership. The success of some groups, indeed, seems to have been due not only to a code, but to the dominant and uncompromising character of the men who administered it for a long time. Often, however, associations have no administrators for the task, or part-time committees which change frequently so that there is no continuity. Often, too, the committees, being peers of the man to be judged, are loath to be strict with a fellow worker. These facts must be faced squarely, if code administration is to have even the limited effectiveness of which it is capable.

In the long run, of course, real success will depend on the development of an enlightened social sense and an *esprit de corps* in the various segments of business. This in its turn can best be promoted by increasing efforts to professionalize business, even though it may never become a full-fledged profession. The traditional professions sometimes took centuries to arrive at a sense of their mission and responsibility. History shows that the task is difficult, but it also proves that it is feasible.

Notes

1. *Cf.* Richard Eells, *The Meaning of Modern Business* (Columbia University Press, 1960), pp. 50 ff. on the metrocorporation; *cf.* Francis X. Sutton, Seymour E. Harris, Carl Kaysen and James Tobin, *The American Business Creed* (Harvard University Press, 1956), pp. 33-36 and pp. 354-368, on the managerial as opposed to the classic business creed.

2. This is clear not only from interviews but from the controversies which appear in the trade press from time to time.

3. J. Whitney Bunting, "The Professionalization of Business," in J. W. Bunting (ed.), *Ethics for Modern Business Practice* (Prentice Hall, 1953), p. 221.

4. *Cf.* Robert A. Brady, *Business as a System of Power* (Columbia University Press, 1943).

5. *Cf.* Lowell Mason, *The Language of Dissent* (World Publishing Co., 1959), for documentation of the problem.

6. *Cf.* Research Institute of America, Report of February 24, 1962, p. 1. *Cf.* Benjamin M. Selekman, "Cynicism and Managerial Morality," in E. Bursk (ed.), *Religion and Business* (Harper and Brothers, 1959), p. 67, and Raymond Baumhart, "How Ethical Are Businessmen?" *Harvard Business Review,* July-August, 1961 (vol. 39, no. 4), p. 19 and pp. 136-158.

7. *Cf.* James S. Hays and Jack L. Ratzkin, "Trade Association Practices and Antitrust Law," *Harvard Business Review,* Summer, 1947, pp. 501-520; *cf. Printers' Ink,* February 10, 1956, p. 27, for some interesting details of the consent decree signed by the American Association of Advertising Agencies.

8. *Cf.* Brady, *op. cit.*

9. *Cf.* R. M. MacIver, "The Social Significance of Professional Ethics" in *The Annals of the American Academy of Political and Social Science,* vol. 297, January 1955, p. 118.

10. Baumhart, *op. cit.,* pp. 168-171.

11. James Melvin Lee, *Business Ethics* (Ronald Press, 1926), p. 176.

12. D. L. Munby, *Christianity and Economic Problems* (London: Macmillan, 1956), p. 174.

13. *Cf.* Benson Y. Landis, *Professional Codes* (Teachers College, Columbia University, 1927), p. 96.

14. The Chamber of Commerce's *Principles of Business Conduct* consists of one sheet of paper containing fifteen short statements. First issued in June 1924, and reissued in June 1961, these principles are so little known that even executives of the Chamber did not know what I wanted when I asked for a copy in August of 1961. The NAB *TV Code,* on the other hand, is a fair-sized booklet which is revised frequently to cover new problems.

15. Chester I. Barnard, "Elementary Conditions of Business Morals," In *California Management Review,* Fall, 1959 (vol. 1, no. 1), p. 4.

16. Harold L. Johnson, *Explorations in Responsible Business Behavior; An Exercise in Behavioral Economics,* Research Paper no. 4, Bureau of Business and Economic Research, School of Business Administration, Georgia State College of Business Administration, 1958, p. 65.

17. Business Ethics Advisory Council, *A Statement of Business Ethics* (U.S. Department of Commerce, 1962).

18. The AMA has two mimeographed folders of codes. One printed in April of 1962 contains sample company policies; the other, dated June 1962, contains association codes.

19. *Cf.* Max Radin, *Manners and Morals of Business* (Bobbs-Merrill, 1939), p. 217.

20. Peter F. Drucker, *The Practice of Management* (Harper and Brothers, 1954), p. 157.

12 BY WAY OF CONCLUSION

DESPITE THE DIVERSITY of topics treated in these pages, certain themes run through the entire book. The most basic is the insistence that business must realize that it has ethical problems, of both an individual and social nature. This should lead naturally to a recognition that businessmen must devote time and effort to the study of these questions: which in turn will broaden the executive's understanding of business, both in its human and social dimensions. Such study and understanding should also sharpen the manager's sense of responsibility for his own competence.

Finally, business will have to recognize that it cannot discharge many of its obligations except through professional groups or in cooperation with organs of the larger society.

Lest these obligations seem too burdensome, most chapters have attempted to show that in a large number of cases the demands of good ethics and of good business are, in practice, identical. It is the contention of this book that many problems need not arise if the business man has an enlightened vision of what will actually contribute to the long-range health of the business community.

At nearly every turn, it has been necessary to point out that the improvement of business ethics depends on the work of the school and the church. This point has been stressed, since so

many leaders in these institutions have used business as a scape-
goat for their own sins of omission. This is all the more serious
because certain intellectuals take up the cry, and suggest solving
the problem by passing the responsibility on to the government.
This, too, is an example of narrow and even reactionary thinking,
based on a cramped ideal of the available possibilities for both
institutional and human reform.

By way of summary and as a first step to increasing personal
awareness of all that is involved, two lists are appended as example examinations of conscience. The first is for business men,
especially for managers. The second should be used by everyone
who is aware that a man's personal integrity influences everything he does.

The Religious Dimension

Principles may guide conscience and check lists may stir it
up, but motivation is still needed. Realistically, it must be admitted that enlightened self-interest and purely rational considerations are often not enough to move men to virtue. Most of us
require a truly religious motivation to enrich, reinforce and
supplement the convictions of unaided reason. In short, the
certitudes of faith are needed to complete the work of ethics.

Men, unlike angels, exist in time. The present moment hyp-
notizes us and shortens our perspectives. As a result, we are
tempted to cut corners and to succumb to petty temptations.
Religious faith counteracts this by putting us in the perspective of
eternity. Within this, we must answer the divine question which
tests the meaning of our lives. "What does it profit a man if he
gains the whole world and suffers the loss of his soul?" This is a
piercing question, and the businessman should ask it every day,
lest he find that his balance sheet is not good enough for
eternity.

Faith can help us to transcend the temptations of the moment, but hope is necessary if man is to vanquish the discouragement of day to day living. Even though virtue is its own reward, the reward is not always immediately visible in this world. The evil often prosper in the short run, and the good, or at least those who try to be noble, are not sure of success at every instant. Worse yet, the apathy of those around us is a constant invitation to give up and to compromise with the world as it is. Only a hope grounded on the promises of God can keep men going in this atmosphere.

Charity, the greatest of the theological virtues, must be the final source of strength in business dealings as in all other spheres of life. It alone can urge men to go beyond the minimum, beyond the strictly obligatory and beyond the short focus of enlightened self-interest. Charity is the corrective for an ethics that is, because it comes from unaided reason, too legalistic perhaps, too timid or too dry and rationalistic. Charity is the antidote for a spirit of calculating expediency. Charity is, or should be, the force which breathes life and holiness back into the decisions of mere men. It must be and do all those wondrous things of which St. Paul writes in I Corinthians 13, vv4-7:

Charity is patient, is kind; charity does not envy, is not pretentious, is not puffed up, is not ambitious, is not self-seeking, is not provoked; thinks no evil, does not rejoice over wickedness, but rejoices with the truth; bears with all things, believes all things, hopes all things, endures all things.

It is this spirit which enables man to accept the burden of existence and to face the task of changing the world into a more perfect reflection of its Creator. In practice, it is only when we labor in the sight of God and under His providence that we can rescue work and life itself from meaninglessness. Granted that we are all unprofitable servants, faith, hope and charity can give us a sense of vocation and the assurance that our feeble efforts in time are pleasing to God, who has given us a world to transform.

CHECK LIST NUMBER ONE

GENERAL:

1. Have I ever given *serious* consideration to the meaning of my work?
    a) Its significance for my own human development?
    b) Its significance for my fellow workers and employees?
    c) Its significance for those who depend on my company?
    d) Its significance for society?

2. Have I ever given *serious* consideration to my responsibilities to each of the groups affected by my work?
    a) Have I dodged my responsibilities by "buck-passing"?
    b) Have I dodged responsibility by using slogans and rationalizations?

3. Have I done anything to discharge my responsibilities?
    a) By isolating problems and working out principles and policies to cover them?
    b) By increasing my competence and understanding of business?
    c) By modifying those conditions which cause problems?
    d) By active membership in business associations?

PARTICULAR:

1. Do I feel and show a real respect for the human dignity of those who work with and for me?

   a) Have I violated my employees right to privacy and to their home life?
   b) Have I avoided responsibility for hiring and firing by hiding behind "scientific" tests and slogans?

2. Have I ever seriously considered the impact of my decisions on society, the local community and business in general?
   a) Are any of my business practices such that if widespread they would seriously harm any of these groups?
   b) Have I paid my taxes honestly?
   c) Have I hidden behind the excuses of the classical business creed?

3. Have I fulfilled my duties to the company for which I work?
   a) Have I neglected the development of human productivity?
   b) Have I allowed short-range considerations to block long-range success?
   c) Have I tolerated practices which, though "accepted," do not contribute to the real good of the firm?

CHECK LIST NUMBER TWO

"WHAT'S YOUR INTEGRITY QUOTIENT?"

Raymond J. Murphy
America, August 18, 1962.

YOUR BUSINESS RELATIONSHIPS:

1. Do you violate proper office-hour procedure by arriving late, leaving early, or by taking lengthy lunch periods or coffee breaks?
2. Do you pad your business expense accounts by overstating mileage, hotel, food, telephone items, etc.?
3. Do you participate in business practices that might be classified as "kickbacks," "under-the-table payments" or "bribing"?
4. Have you ever claimed credit at work for the ideas or labors of someone else?
5. Do you "borrow" stamps from the office supply for personal use and then forget to pay for them or to replace them?
6. Have you received benefits through improper reporting relative to welfare relief, unemployment or workmen's compensation, or GI dependency?
7. Have you placed the blame on someone else for your own mistakes at work?

8. Do you use company time or facilities (telephone, car, office, etc.) for personal business?

9. Do you pass off most of your responsibility to colleagues to free yourself for your own personal pursuits?

10. Have you assisted anyone at work (yourself included) in becoming a "draftdodger"? In skipping jury duty?

11. Do you take "approved leaves," ostensibly for company business or sickness, when in fact they are for personal reasons?

12. Do you entertain (at the theatre, sports, etc.), or give gifts to your personal friends or family, and then charge it to business expense?

13. Do you ever claim credit for overtime work at the office or for time spent away from the office "on business," when in fact it is otherwise?

14. Do you knowingly order merchandise for a specific purpose and then return it after it has served its purpose?

15. Do you take home and keep office supplies or equipment for your personal use?

16. Have you knowingly accepted overpayment in change from merchants without returning it?

YOUR PRIVATE RELATIONSHIPS:

1. Have you claimed income-tax deductions by improperly listing a child, parent or other dependent?

2. Have you cheated at sports, such as tennis, golf, etc., or at cards, crossword puzzles, etc.?

3. Do you try to beat traffic laws through speeding, illegal turns, parking violations, etc.?

4. Do you shortchange the government on your income-tax return by overstating charitable deductions, interest payments, retail taxes paid, medical payments, etc.?

5. Have you used connections to "fix" traffic violations?

6. Are you a "seat jumper" at theatres, sport events, etc. (buy a $2 seat, but occupy a $4 seat)?

7. Do you sometimes connect your outside home electrical appliances, water, etc., to your neighbors' outlets?

8. Do you cheat your spouse by overstating home-operating expenses (for women) or normal incidental work expenses (for men)?

9. Do you frequently use someone else's automobile without any thought of paying for or replacing the gas used?

JACKPOT QUESTION:

Have you answered any of the above questions with a "no," when in your heart you know it should be "yes"?

Scoreboard: "Yes" answers to questions in either group (plus the Jackpot Question) should be rated thus:

0	A	(Excellent)
1-2	B	(Fair)
3-4	C	(Weak but satisfactory)
5-over	D	(Failure)